Sut
Pl

Mly

THE OTHER
MITFORD

DIANA ALEXANDER

THE OTHER MITFORD

Pamela's Story

For Malcolm who has constantly encouraged me in this project.

For Kate and Emily, who knew and loved Pam, and for Daisy and Ruby who would have loved her had they known her.

First published 2012

The History Press
The Mill, Brimscombe Port
Stroud, Gloucestershire, GL5 2QG
www.thehistorypress.co.uk

© Diana Alexander, 2012

The right of Diana Alexander to be identified as the Author
of this work has been asserted in accordance with the
Copyrights, Designs and Patents Act 1988.

British Library Cataloguing in Publication Data.
A catalogue record for this book is available from the British Library.

ISBN 978 0 7524 7121 1

Typesetting and origination by The History Press
Printed in Great Britain

Contents

Foreword

by Jonathan Guinness

'This is my sister Pam,' said Deborah Devonshire as I introduced a friend to them both. 'She's just back from Switzerland and she·can tell you the menu of every meal she's had on the way.' For Pam was legendary for never forgetting food. Her symbol in Charlotte Mosley's collection of the six sisters' letters, corresponding to Unity's swastika, Jessica's hammer and sickle and so on, is crossed spoons. Perhaps this was the occasion when Pam had brought to Chatsworth in her luggage a dozen eggs which when hatched would grow into the elegantly coiffed Appenzeller Spitzhaube chickens which were then new to this country.

Until now Pam has been the only one of the six Mitford sisters not to be the subject of a book to herself, and in filling this gap Diana Alexander has, as it were, earthed the Mitford story. 'My wife is normal,' wailed Lord Redesdale. 'I am normal, but my daughters are all off their heads.' Well, not all, actually. Pam could run a farm or a household to perfection: she coped for thirteen years with a millionaire husband who was physics professor, steeplechase jockey, and air ace but also dangerously mercurial and liable to behave outrageously. Their marriage broke up but he retained deep fondness for her through four later marriages, leaving her a fortune in his will.

In managing Derek, Pam perhaps benefitted from having suffered from Nancy as her older sister. For Nancy was an accomplished tease and Pam, as next oldest, was the one who bore the brunt. But Nancy was also very funny, and what Pam and the others all learned was to ride with the punch, to enjoy the jokes without being too upset by the unkindness.

Pam's childhood polio certainly set her back educationally, but I'm not sure she was dyslexic. If so, it was a very mild case. She was a rather erratic speller, but so was Evelyn Waugh. She was not as avid a reader as the others, but *Tales of Old Japan* was not the only one of her Redesdale grandfather's books she absorbed: she knew them all, including his substantial *Memories*. She learned German without having a single lesson and spoke it well enough to guide Nancy through East Germany when Nancy was researching her biography of Frederick the Great.

What I most respected in Pam was her love of the truth. When I told her I was intending to write the story of the Mitfords her first words were: 'Yes: the real story, what actually happened.' She was then endlessly helpful and her reminiscences, never in any way slanted, conveyed a sense of reality that took one back in time. It was this regard for truth that triggered an occasion mentioned in the *Letters* when Pam seems to have lost her temper, a rare event. Diana describes it in a letter to Deborah. Pam had been with Nancy and Jessica who had agreed with each other that the Mitford childhood was miserable. This, Pam had said indignantly, was quite untrue, and as she told the story to Diana she flushed and there were tears in her eyes.

Pam was always there when needed. She was staunch when Diana was clapped into Holloway without trial at what is supposed to have been Britain's finest hour; she immediately took in Diana's two babies and their Nanny. Then many years later, when Nancy was dying and all the sisters took turn at looking after her, it was always Pam whom she most wanted. When she herself was growing old, her many friends and relations loved the stories she told and her sense of humour, less sophisticated perhaps than that of her sisters, was always fun. Diana Alexander gives us a good taste of it.

Introduction

So much has been written about the Mitford sisters, both by others and by themselves, that it would seem unlikely there is much left to say. It is incredible, therefore, that one of the sisters is still virtually unknown and there has certainly never been anything published in which she is the central figure – until now.

Pamela was the second of the six 'Mitford Girls' – a phrase coined by future poet laureate John Betjeman – and she had a tough childhood owing to the jealousy of her elder sister Nancy, who bitterly resented the new baby. Pamela had polio as a child which held back her physical progress; she was also probably dyslexic, a condition which was not recognised at the beginning of the twentieth century and was the reason why she was the only one of the sisters – apart from Unity, whose suicide attempt put paid to any authorship by her – who never wrote a book.

Pamela was a superb cook, a knowledgeable farmer and an imaginative gardener but, most important of all, she was the member of this extraordinary family who most resembled her mother, Lady Redesdale, whose mantle she gradually assumed, picking up the family pieces – and there were many – being there when help was needed and bringing the practical side of her nature to bear on the others' problems.

Unlike most of the sisters she never espoused a cause, never brought any grief to her parents and, together with her youngest sister Deborah, was the only one who would have admitted to a happy childhood; and this was in spite of the treatment meted out to her by Nancy who also led the other siblings in the often cruel teasing. Of all the sisters she possessed the most contented personality. When, in the 1930s, the other 'gels' were forever in the news, Lady Redesdale once ruefully remarked: 'Whenever I see a headline beginning "Peer's daughter" I know it's going to be about one of you children.' But she wasn't thinking of Pam.

This is not to say that Pam was in any way dull. Her humour was not as sharp but she loved hearing the others' jokes; she could tell a funny story as well as anyone – usually about something which had happened to her – and her memory for past events (particularly meals) was legendary in the family. She never had any children but her nieces and nephews loved her because she never patronised them and was always ready to listen to what they had to say. In a strikingly good-looking family she more than held her own: she had the corn-flower blue eyes inherited from the Mitford side and a face whose serenity not only reflected her personality but made her a close rival to Diana, always known as the beauty of the family. Although the others felt she was not as quick off the mark as they were, clever men were captivated by her. John Betjeman twice proposed to her and was twice rejected and she finally married Derek Jackson, one of the most eminent scientists of his generation, who also became a war hero and a successful amateur jockey. True, they were eventually divorced, but of his six wives she was married to him the longest and they became great friends after their divorce, even causing speculation among the sisters that they might remarry.

In spite of being rather shy, Pam possessed a tremendous spirit of adventure. During the year she spent in France she had a ride in a tank, which she declared was much more exciting than any of the social events to which she was invited and wished she could do it all over again, and during the 1930s she motored alone all over Europe.

Shortly after her marriage to Derek she became one of the first women to fly across the Atlantic in a commercial aircraft, taking it all in her stride. Prior to that she had enjoyed gold-prospecting with her parents in Canada (although this was never a successful enterprise) and later had managed the farm belonging to Bryan Guinness, Diana's first husband.

It was not long after this that she really began to come into her own as the rescuer of her other siblings. During the war she gained much kudos within the family by having the two baby Mosley boys to stay with her and Derek while their parents were in prison for pro-German activities before the war. When Nancy was dying from a particularly painful form of cancer, it was Pam who she wanted with her when the pain was at its worst, and it was also Pam – since she was so practical – who played an important part in looking after Lady Redesdale just before her death.

After her divorce from Derek she went to live in Switzerland, where it was a joke among the sisters that she knew all the Gnomes of Zurich. When she returned finally to England she settled down to a contented old age at Woodfield House in the tiny Cotswold village of Caudle Green, midway between Cheltenham and Cirencester.

It was here that I first met her as I also lived in Caudle Green, and for twelve very happy years I worked as her cleaning lady and also became her friend. When I first arrived at Woodfield House, I had no idea that Pamela Jackson was one of the Mitford sisters and when the penny dropped, I simply could not believe that this lovely, amusing and compassionate lady really was the 'Other' Mitford, and very few people knew it.

I should say here that I was not a professional cleaning lady (though I must have been quite good at it because Pam was something of a perfectionist) but was at home with my young children as they grew up. It was not easy to pursue my previous job as a journalist because childcare was not available in the 1970s as it is today, but I could fit in the cleaning while the children were at school and in the holidays it was a treat for them to come with me because, like all children, they loved Pam.

All the time I was there I realised the unique position I was in and I couldn't wait to write about this missing Mitford. I met her sisters and her friends and I talked to her at length about her life and her family. Apart from short features in magazines, however, there was never time in my busy life to write about her in the detail I felt she so richly deserved. Three years ago I retired from full-time journalism and knew that now was the time. This, then, is the result.

But first, and bearing in mind that the Mitford sisters are still mainly remembered by what is now the older generation – though Nancy's novels have recently been republished, Debo's life story, *Wait for Me*, has received enormous publicity, there are new books about Nancy and Jessica, and the Mitford bandwagon seems to roll on and on – it might be useful to put Pam in context by describing some of the other members of her remarkable and eccentric family.

The Mitford story really starts with the two grandfathers, Algernon Bertram Mitford, the first Lord Redesdale, known as Barty to his family and friends, and Thomas Gibson Bowles, whose nickname was Tap. The Redesdales originated from Northumbria, taking the title name from the village of Redesdale, while Thomas Bowles was the illegitimate but much-loved son of a Liberal politician. Their backgrounds were very different but the two men got on well together, at one time both serving as Conservative Members of Parliament. They are both important in the Mitford story because it was largely from them that the girls who became writers inherited their talents. Barty, who spent some time in the diplomatic service, wrote about his experiences in both China and Japan and his *Tales of Old Japan* became a classic which has seldom been out of print. Tap branched out in a different direction, founding first the magazine *Vanity Fair* and then *The Lady*, which is still going strong today.

You might wonder what these two men had passed on to Pam, who found writing quite taxing, but it was their spirit of adventure which she inherited. Barty travelled to the far-flung corners of the world and numbered explorer Richard Burton among his friends, while Tap was an intrepid sailor who had a master mariner's certificate and, after his wife's untimely death, spent much time at sea, taking his children with him. Pam would not have been out of place in either of those worlds.

It was through the somewhat unlikely friendship of their fathers that David Freeman Mitford and Sydney Bowles first met and their marriage was very much one of opposites. His volatile nature was tempered by the very pronounced sense of humour which he passed on to his children; although they quaked at his rages, all agreed that no one could make them laugh more than him, especially when he and Nancy got together. He loved country life and field sports, especially fishing, but was not good with money, usually selling his properties when prices were low and buying again when they had risen. Sydney, on the other hand, was much more serious, although she too had a good sense of humour. She had kept house for her father since the age of 14 and as a consequence had a very real sense of the value of things and nothing was ever wasted. Nancy and Jessica in particular felt that she was a rather vague and distant mother, and this image of her comes over in the character of Aunt Sadie in Nancy's novels, *The Pursuit of Love* and *Love in a Cold Climate*. They seldom realised how devoted she was to her unruly children and how devastating she found their behaviour as young adults.

Pam inherited her striking good looks and her love of the countryside from her father but, of all the sisters, she was most like Sydney in character, being utterly practical (which the others, except Debo, were not), careful with money, an excellent cook and provider, and, latterly, the one to whom they all turned when they needed help.

Pam's siblings need little introduction since much has been written about them already, but for those not familiar with the Mitford Industry, as the family called it, here are some brief sketches:

Nancy, the eldest of the sisters, was born in 1904. With her dark hair and green eyes she did not inherit the Mitford looks and her sense of humour was more sharp and cruel than that of her siblings. Although she became a very successful writer, she was never quite satisfied with her lot and certainly life dealt her some severe blows. She married Peter Rodd but the marriage was not a success and finally broke up, after which she made her home in France. The great love of her life was Gaston Palewski, one of General de Gaulle's right-hand men. Known in the family as The Col, he is immortalised as Fabrice in *The Pursuit of Love*. Nancy's novels and biographies made her rich but not happy. She will ever be remembered as the creator of U and Non-U (upper-class and non-upper-class speak) in a book called *Noblesse Oblige*.

Tom, the only boy in the family, was born in 1909. He cheerfully put up with his noisy, teasing sisters, partly because of his equable nature and also because he was the only one of the family to go away to boarding school. He was not as pro-Nazi as Diana and Unity, but he was sympathetic to Germany and chose to fight in Burma rather than Europe. He died of wounds in 1945, a tremendous family tragedy, which meant that the Redesdale title passed to a cousin.

Diana, who was only a year younger than Tom – the two were very close as children – was deemed to be the beauty of the family. She couldn't wait to leave home and at the age of 19 married Bryan Guinness, heir to the brewing empire; but later she met Sir Oswald Mosley who became the love of her life. He was forming the British Union of Fascists at the time and Diana became one of his devotees and also one of his mistresses, for faithfulness was not in his nature.

She divorced Bryan and from then on devoted her life to Mosley and his cause, marrying him in secret in Germany in 1936 after the death of his first wife. The Mosleys were imprisoned during the war and afterwards went to live permanently in France. Diana possessed the family gift for writing and as well as reviewing books for various publications, wrote books of her own. Having been deemed by one of her nannies as too beautiful to live, she died aged 93 in the Paris heatwave of 2003, surviving Mosley by more than twenty years but never renouncing his views.

Even in this eccentric family Unity was felt to be unusual. She also inherited her father's good looks – and his height. 'Poor Unity, she is rather huge,' said Lady Redesdale when Unity was fitted for her bridesmaid's dress for Diana's wedding. But it was her physical appearance which first brought her to Hitler's notice, leading to an extraordinary friendship between the daughter of an English country gentleman and the German Führer. Unity's strong opinions led her to attempt suicide in 1939, which left her brain-damaged.

In the family, in spite of the fact that she could be moody and sulky, Unity was loved for her originality, the laughter she generated and the tricks she got up to. Relationships among the sisters fluctuated depending on what stage they had reached or what cause they were supporting at the time, but the close ties between Unity and Jessica never wavered until the outbreak of war and Unity's suicide attempt, which separated them forever. In spite of their totally opposing views, for Jessica espoused the communist cause, they remained firm friends and missed each other badly when those beliefs finally drove them apart. Unity died after an attack of meningitis in 1948.

Even more than Unity, Jessica was a discontented teenager who longed to get away from home and go to boarding school. She ran away to Spain with her cousin Esmond Romilly, who supported the communists in the Spanish Civil War, and later married him. After moving to America, Esmond joined the Royal Canadian Air Force on the outbreak of war but was lost on a mission over the North Sea. Jessica later married Bob Treuhaft and became a member of the Communist Party and a campaigner for civil rights. After the success of her autobiographical book *Hons and Rebels*, she was able to make a career out of writing. Always the rebel, she remained almost permanently at odds with the rest of her family, yet she kept in touch with all her sisters, except Diana. She died of cancer in 1996.

Deborah (or Debo) never gave her family cause for anxiety. She was a happy child who openly loved her parents but her birth was not greeted with great joy since her parents were still hoping for another boy. She eventually wrote several books, mainly about Chatsworth House, which became her home, culminating in her acclaimed biography *Wait for Me*.

Debo married Lord Andrew Cavendish, who succeeded as Duke of Devonshire when his elder brother was killed in the war, and they inherited Chatsworth – and a lot of death duties. That these were paid off and that Chatsworth is now probably the leading privately owned stately home open to the public is in huge measure down to Debo's enormous energy and imagination.

In spite of her optimistic and equable nature, she, too, endured tragedy since she had three stillborn babies and another that died shortly after birth; she did, however, produce Peregrine, the present Duke of Devonshire, Emma and Sophia. In later life she became the family peacemaker, which was not an easy task.

The sisters' high-profile lifestyles were further enhanced by their equally high-profile family and friends. They were cousins of the Churchills, related to former prime minister Harold Macmillan and numbered most of the literary figures of their generation among their friends. Diana was probably the only person in the world to be friendly with both Churchill and Hitler, and she and Unity knew most of the German High Command. Debo's friends included Ali Khan, the Kennedy family, Prince Charles and the late Queen Mother.

Since there were sixteen years between Nancy and Debo, the sisters spanned an unusual and changing swathe of history: the eldest three were born as the long, easy-going Edwardian afternoon was drawing to a close and when Britain still ruled over a vast empire on which it seemed the sun would never set; Unity when the lights were going out all over Europe; Jessica when the 'war to end all wars' was in its final stages; and Debo at the beginning of the roaring twenties. They witnessed changes of the sort that had never been seen before – women's suffrage, Irish Home Rule, the General Strike, the Slump and yet another war; and they all lived to see a world which had changed beyond recognition from the one into which they were born. But they have never lost their popularity, in spite of the generations who have never heard of the Mitford sisters, and Nancy's novels still fly off the shelves of leading booksellers. Even Andrew Marr saw fit to devote a section of his excellent history *The Making of Modern Britain* to this extraordinary family.

It is tempting to ask 'why?' Many devotees will have their different reasons and many theories have been advanced by those more qualified to speculate on the phenomenon of the Mitford family. My task is to tell the story of Pam who, because she never sought the limelight, has somehow fallen below the radar. I hope to show that in her quiet and understated way, she was just as interesting as her more flamboyant siblings.

Nicknames

Most families have nicknames for at least some of their members, but all the Mitford family had a series of names which they called one another at different times. I have by no means used all of them, but most of them are worth listing if only to show their diversity.

Nancy was called Koko in early childhood by both her parents and her father sometimes called her Blob-Nose. Her older siblings, Pam, Tom and Diana, called her Naunce or Naunceling; Jessica called her Susan; and after she went to live in France, Debo would refer to her as the French Lady Writer, the Old French Lady or simply Lady.

Practical Pam was always known as Woman to the others, who also called her Wooms or Woomling.

Tom was Tud or Tuddemy, which stood for Tom in Boudledidge, the secret language made up by Unity and Jessica.

Diana was Dina to her father while her mother called her Dana. She had a rather large head as a child so Nancy called her Bodley, short for The Bodley Head; she was Nard or Nardy to Pam, Tom and Unity; Jessica called her Cord or Corduroy; while to Debo she was always Honks. History does not relate where these last three nicknames originated.

Unity was most often called Bobo, a derivative of Baby, which her parents called her when she was small. She and Jessica called each other Boud (pronounced Bowd), presumably because they were the only two speakers of Boudledidge. Diana and Jessica took to calling her Birdie, a derivative of Boud. Not many people actually called her Unity – except Hitler.

Jessica quickly became Decca, though her mother called her Little D; Nancy called her Susan, and Jessica and Debo called each other Hen or Henderson, partly on account of their devotion to poultry. Occasionally, and mysteriously, she was called Squalor; equally mysterious was Pam's nickname for her of Steake, pronounced Ste-ake.

Debo was called Stubby during her early years by her mother, on account of her (compared to the others') stubby little legs. Pam changed this to Stublow, which she used at intervals for the rest of her life when writing to her youngest sister. Nancy often called her Miss or Nine, telling her that this referred to her mental age. On one occasion Debo, having written an unusually long letter to Nancy, ended by saying that if she didn't finish soon Nancy would be forced to change her name to Ten.

The children called their father Farve and their mother Muv, but also referred to them as TPOM (The Poor Old Male) and TPOF (The Poor Old Female). Sydney was also known as Fem or the Fem. The children thought these names were very much their preserve, but one day Sydney was telephoned by Violet Hammersley (one of the family's oldest friends, and christened The Wid by the children since she always wore mourning clothes after her husband's death), and she instantly recognised the gloomy voice. Forgetting herself entirely, Sydney said, 'Hello Wid'; 'Hello Fem' was the instant reply. David and Sydney were also known jointly as The Revereds.

Those who married into the family were given nicknames, too. Nancy's husband Peter Rodd became Prod and her lover, Gaston Palewski, was known as The Colonel or Col; Derek Jackson who married Pam was Horse; Oswald Mosley was Sir O, Sir Oz, Sir Ogre, the Leader or Kit, which was Diana's pet name for him; Debo's husband Andrew, Duke of Devonshire, was sometimes known as Claud on account of his receiving letters mistakenly addressed to Claud Hartington Esq., when his title, before he inherited his father's, was Lord Hartington.

It is fortunate that the absolutely excellent *The Mitfords: Letters Between Six Sisters* – correspondence between the Mitford Girls over a period of almost eighty years – was edited by Charlotte Mosley, a member of the family by marriage. At least she could refer to Debo, the last surviving sister, when sorting out this plethora of nicknames.

One

Not an Easy Childhood

'Another beautiful little girl, sir!' said the midwife to the handsome man with the fair hair and piercing blue eyes, who stood by his wife's bedside as she was safely delivered of their second child. The year was 1907 and the most unusual aspect of this birth was that the father was actually present, as he was at the births of all his seven children. Although he may have hoped for a boy to carry on the family name, he was not unduly perturbed. His wife was a healthy young woman; there would be more opportunities for a son.

Had he been able to look into the future, the Hon. David Freeman Mitford would have had much to worry about for he would have seen that he and his wife Sydney would produce four more girls and only one boy, Tom; and this son would be killed at the end of the second great conflict to engulf the century which had only just begun. Most of his girls would become famous or infamous during their lifetime: two would be well-known writers, two would become high-profile friends of Hitler and one would marry a duke. One of the writers would run away with her cousin to fight for the communists in Spain and one of the Nazi sympathisers would try to kill herself. Even if he had had a crystal ball and seen what was ahead for his large family, would he have believed it? In his case the truth was to be far stranger than fiction.

For the moment he need not have worried, for the child which he was shortly to hold in his arms was the one who would never cause trouble. If a fairy godmother was present at her birth, she endowed this baby, Pamela, not only with beauty – she had her father's fair hair and bright blue eyes – but also with a nature so agreeable and coura-geous that she was able to weather the many storms of life which were to befall her and her exceptional family. Although she did not have his volatile temper, Pam, more so than her siblings, took after her father, in the sense that she never craved the bright lights of city life and was most at home in the heart of the English countryside. Often in conflict with his other daughters, except Deborah the youngest, he and Pam seldom disagreed and she avoided the brunt of his tower-ing rages. The fairy godmother had done her work well – but she had reckoned without Pam's elder sister, the dark-haired, green-eyed, sharp-witted Nancy.

Nancy famously remarked that the first three years of her life were perfect. 'Then a terrible thing happened, my sister Pamela was born.' She claimed that it put her into a permanent rage for about twenty years. What initially upset her most was that the nanny of the time immediately transferred her affections to the new baby and Nancy was heard by her mother to say: 'Oh Ninny, how I wish you could still love me!' When nanny was sent away as a result she became even more sad, since she realised, even at such a young age, that she was in some way responsible for the dismissal.

Ironically, Pam was the least likely of any of Nancy's sisters to cause her pain or provide any sibling rivalry. The fact that she was not so quick-witted has often been blamed on a severe bout of polio which struck her down at the age of 3, but she was possibly also dyslexic – a condition not then recognised. Her kindness, which Nancy only acknowledged much later in life, was an inbuilt part of her nature.

In 1911 polio or infantile paralysis was a dreaded illness which, if it did not kill, could leave the sufferer severely paralysed for life. This posed a big problem for Pam's mother Sydney, later Lady Redesdale, who had inherited from her father, Thomas Gibson Bowles, theories on the medical profession which were highly unconventional, especially a century ago.

She believed implicitly in the power of the Good Body to heal itself. She banned, as far as possible, all medicines and would call in a doctor only in the most dire emergency. Any medicine which he did provide was left untouched in a cupboard. None of the children were vaccinated, although vaccination was well on the way to becoming compulsory. Pam, however, was so ill that her mother was forced to call in six doctors, one after the other, all of whom told the same story – nothing could be done for the desperately sick little girl. She then contacted the only medical practitioner that she had ever trusted.

Dr Kellgren came from Sweden and specialised in osteopathy, a branch of medicine not to be recognised as mainstream for many decades. Massage and exercise, an early form of intense physiotherapy, were his prescriptions for a cure. And they worked. Pam's recovery was so nearly complete (she was left with a slight weakness in her right leg for the rest of her life) that she was able to ride, swim, skate and even ski. Dr Kellgren's methods were not unique but they were rare for the time and all her life Pam attributed this near miracle entirely to him.

Sydney then applied Dr Kellgren's maxims to all injuries and Jessica, the second youngest of the sisters, in her book *Hons and Rebels*, tells of the time she broke her arm: after the doctor had set it and bound it up, her mother removed all the bandages and made Jessica do exercises to prevent the arm becoming stiff. This was the treatment Sydney herself had received for a broken ankle many years before and it had worked. It succeeded for Jessica too, although it left her somewhat double-jointed. Although some of Jessica's accounts of her childhood must be taken with the proverbial pinch of salt, this one has a ring of truth about it.

In the short term, the illness left Pam in considerable pain and she was often tearful. With a gap of only three years, Nancy and Pam could have become good friends and playmates, but Pam couldn't keep up with Nancy, either mentally or physically, and the problem was compounded by Nancy constantly being told: 'You've got to be nice to Pam, she's ill.'

This state of affairs had two results: Pam became the main butt of Nancy's cruel teasing and she spent a lot of her childhood on her own or playing with the next two younger children, Tom and Diana. She and Diana had secret houses and played endless games together but there were times when Pam was alone and seemed rather left out. She was never self-pitying but would often go for walks by herself – possibly to get away from Nancy's teasing. 'When I was walking on my own today I found a penny. Wasn't I lucky?' she once said. That would appeal to the little girl who was to become something of a family joke for most of her life for her 'careful' attitude towards money. Due to her illness, as well as the three-year age gap, she was well behind Nancy when it came to learning so she was taught with Tom and Diana.

Pam went to dancing class with Tom, where their teacher was Miss Vacani who taught upper-class children their first dancing steps for more than thirty years. Tom, who danced in green shoes with silver buckles, was a great favourite of Miss Vacani, but poor Pam after having polio could not hop on her right leg. She was not able to dance the polka and was kept in the back row and largely disregarded. As ever, she seems to have taken no offence at this lack of attention. Maybe she was just getting used to it and developing a veneer of 'not minding' which was to serve her well in later life.

Like the other children Pam had a great love of animals, and for her – and later her youngest sister Debo – this lasted for her entire life. Jessica describes how Pam spent considerable time pretending to be a horse, pawing the ground, tossing her head and neighing in a most realistic manner – presumably having closely observed the ponies which all the children rode.

In *Hons and Rebels* Jessica remarks that Pam eventually gave up wanting to be a horse and did the next best thing by marrying a jockey. Pam's husband, Derek Jackson, happened to be a very competent amateur jockey and rode several times in the Grand National. He was also a renowned physicist and a war hero who was decorated for his service as a bomber navigator in the RAF.

Pam's love of animals and the countryside was undoubtedly a buffer against the teasing from her siblings, especially Nancy. Alone among the children, except for Debo, who was thirteen years her junior (the two became the closest of the sisters in later life), she was perfectly content with country life and never hankered for the endless socialising which obsessed Nancy, Diana and Jessica. Although as children all the sisters were mad about animals, the incident involving Brownie, the pony which their father bought at Harrods and transported to their London home in a hansom cab, gave Pam particular pleasure. Even more exciting was the journey back to High Wycombe where the family had rented a house. When the pony was not allowed to travel in the guard's van, David refused to be thwarted and transferred the whole family from first to third class (in those days, as today, third-class carriages did not have a corridor) and parents, children, servants and pony travelled home together. The children were particularly thrilled to be able to travel third class – a novelty for upper-class children in those days.

Due to the weakness in her leg from her attack of polio, Pam could not go hunting because she could not get a good enough grip on the saddle to enable her to jump. But she loved riding and adored Charles Hooper the groom, who was in charge of the children's riding activities. He was 'sweet Hoops' to Pam and 'Choops' to the others – and again it shows Pam's kindly and optimistic disposition because sweet was something which Mr Hooper certainly was not. Somewhat grumpy in the first place, his nature had not been improved by the time he spent in the trenches in the Great War, where he suffered from shellshock, and his temper became such that he often exploded without warning. He judged everyone on their riding ability and on nothing else, but he must have realised how hard Pam had to work to ride properly because his temper was seldom vented on her. Nancy, who rode well and was also a favourite, based the character of Josh, the groom in *The Pursuit of Love*, on Hooper.

An extraordinary event happened when Hooper was delivering the eggs from Sydney's chicken farm on 11 November 1927, nine years after the end of the Great War, memories of which were still very vivid in people's minds. Then, as today, the two minutes' silence was observed on the actual date of Armistice Day and Hooper, the old soldier, stopped the cart at 11 a.m. and climbed down to hold the horse's head. The horse, a mare that had seen service with the army in France during the war, swayed in the shafts and fell down dead, probably from a heart attack. Her death, during the two minutes' silence, made a great impression on the Mitford family and crusty old Hooper wept for her.

Yet although the Mitford girls loved their animals, and would weep copiously if they were hurt or in pain, their attitude did not extend to their beloved hens. Pam would often reminisce about Sunday lunch at Asthall or Swinbrook when the roast chicken appeared. 'Is this Blackie or Whitey we're eating today?' one of the children would ask, but she did not remember anyone being put off their lunch when the meat was identified.

Even during her childhood Pam was honing the skills of gardening, animal husbandry and cooking which were partly responsible for her being nicknamed Woman by her siblings. It was also her serenity, her care for others and her capable kindness which made the name stick and which gave her a special place in this extraordinary family.

Pam had her own brand of humour which, though different from her siblings, was still extremely funny. In much later life, when living in the Cotswold village of Caudle Green, Pam and I were invited to supper with our great friend Mary Sager who also lived in the village. The purpose was to meet a newcomer, one Dr Ezra, who had just rented a nearby cottage. Dr Ezra, an American, was full of lengthy advice on most subjects. The first topic of the evening was education and the newcomer delivered a long and stern lecture on schools, many and various, both in England and across the pond. But even she had to stop eventually to draw breath and Pam, quick as a flash, leaned across the table and announced in her unmistakable 'Mitford voice': 'I never went to school, you know.' It was the last time education was mentioned that evening. In fact, in spite of Nancy's descriptions of the Radlett family's sketchy education in her novels, the Mitford children were soundly taught first by Sydney, and later by a series of governesses, Miss Mirams and Miss Hussey being the most competent.

Pam lagged behind her siblings in the classroom, but she was nobody's fool, as is shown particularly by two incidents during her childhood. The first, when she did her best to avert disaster, happened during the Great War when the family was staying with Sydney's father at his cottage on the Solent. At bedtime Pam declared that she could smell smoke but the nursery maid took no notice, thinking that she was making an excuse to stay up longer. David returned on leave two days later to discover that the building had been burnt to the ground. Luckily, no one was hurt and the family had decamped to the home of their neighbour Mr Marconi, the radio pioneer. The children regarded the fire as a great adventure as they sat on the lawn watching the blaze, the grown-ups hurrying backwards and forwards trying to save what they could. Six-year-old Tom, always known for his politeness, called out, 'Good morning, Mr Caddick' to the butler as he hurried past with a load of dining-room silver, and was surprised not to get an answer. Even at such a tender age, Pam had reason to indulge in feelings of self-righteousness.

On another occasion a big fete was being held in the grounds of Batsford Park in aid of a nearby convalescent home for the war-wounded. Sydney, thinking that the popular white elephant stall was looking somewhat bare, took several 'knick-knacks' from the house to fill the empty spaces. Among these was a very rare Buddha collected by her father-in-law, the first Lord Redesdale, during his Far Eastern travels. Sydney thought it was ugly but it was valuable even then. Pam bought it for sixpence and treasured it to the end of her life.

Pam's youngest sister Debo, when interviewed quite recently, put forward the idea that when they were growing up they had far more freedom than today's children and were not constantly supervised by adults. It was when they became young women that they were chaperoned. Pam states that, unlike her father and his siblings, they were allowed to play with the village children and the only time she ever got into trouble for doing so was when she stayed out after dark and a search party had to be organised. Indoors the children had the run of the house, in this case Batsford Park with its five staircases, in which to play hide and seek to their hearts' content. In these games they were often joined by David and their grandmother Clementine, not to supervise them but to join in the general hilarity. On one occasion,

Grandmother Redesdale fell flat on her back and it was thought that it was only the bun on the back of her head that saved her from serious concussion.

One of the games, inevitably invented by Nancy, was a variation on 'doctors and nurses' in which Nancy would play the part of a 'Czechish' lady doctor. She spoke with the heavy foreign accent which she imagined an inhabitant of Czechoslovakia would use. Tom was generally the patient, Diana his anxious mother and Pam the nurse. An instant and serious 'opairation' was embarked upon, usually involving a painful knuckling of the chest. It was during this game that Czechish, the first of the Mitfords' private languages, was begun and Nancy used it to the end of her life.

It was at this time that Pam's nickname Woman often became Woomling and Nancy would say of her, 'Oh, she ees wondairful', sometimes also referring to her simply as Wondairful or Wondair. Nancy, as a result of this game, was often referred to as Naunceling or Naunce, especially by Pam. It is the final irony that when Nancy was dying a particularly painful death from cancer and Pam was the sister she most wanted to look after her due to her quiet, capable attitude, she would write to the other sisters to say, 'Woomling ees wondair', or simply, 'she ees, she ees'. They knew what she meant.

In common with other upper-class children of their day, the Mitford children saw comparatively little of their parents and much more of their nanny and governess. Lily Kersey, the nanny who blotted her copybook by her treatment of Nancy after Pam was born, an unkindness which affected Pam at least equally, was succeeded by Norah Evans of whom nothing is known. In her wake came the Unkind Nanny who was briefly with the family around the time of Diana's birth and made the remark, which went down in Redesdale family history: 'She's too beautiful. She can't live long.' In fact, Diana died aged 93. The Unkind Nanny was sacked, ostensibly for banging Nancy's head against a wooden bedpost, though Nancy said she did not remember this. True or not, her departure led to the Redesdales engaging a nanny who made a tremendous difference to their children's lives and who devoted her own life to them.

Laura Dicks, who became known as Blor, was pale and thin and Sydney wondered if she would be capable of looking after the boisterous Mitford children. But she also exclaimed over Diana's beauty and was engaged on the spot. The difference between her and the other nannies was that she was scrupulously fair and so was loved by all, even Nancy. Her background was Nonconformist but, far from being dour, she was both charming and funny. Nancy said of herself that, although she was still vile to the others, she would have been much worse but for Blor. Her influence on Nancy must have made Pam's life a little easier and, like all the others, Pam loved Blor dearly.

Blor stayed with the family for more than thirty years and during this time she often took the children on holiday to her home at Bexhill-on-Sea in Sussex; there they enjoyed the delights of sea bathing, after which Blor would rub their freezing limbs with dry, striped towels and give them ginger biscuits and hot drinks from her Thermos.

In his book *The House of Mitford*, the definitive history of this exceptional family, Jonathan Guinness, Diana's eldest son, acknowledges the tremendous help that his mother and his aunt Debo gave him with his research. But he remarks that, 'as with most of us, their memory of the past is selected, packaged, interpreted. Pam does very little of this; her memories, as she recalls them, retain the freshness of direct perception.' One of the best examples of this is Pam's descriptions of childhood Christmases, which in old age she recounted to me as if they were yesterday.

Preparations for the great event began in October when Sydney started making Christmas shopping trips to Oxford – never London – to buy presents for the tree from Elliston and Cavell and the children's favourite shop, Hooton's bazaar. By the end of November they began to pack the parcels, a mammoth task since there was a present for every adult who worked on the estate and a garment for each of their children. Many of the clothes had been knitted by Sydney earlier in the year. Every child also took home an orange and a bag of sweets from the Christmas tree. It was Pam's job to wrap up the sweets in home-made bags and she always wished that she could eat them all herself.

On Christmas Eve a huge tree from the estate was brought in and decorated by the family. Then all the uncles, aunts and cousins arrived, amid great excitement. Next there was tea for a hundred guests from the estate, followed by the arrival of Father Christmas to the sound of 'sleigh bells'. David would fling open the door to admit the scarlet-clad figure with his sack bulging with presents. It was years before the Mitford children solved the puzzle of why the parson, Mr Foster, was the only guest who came late to the party, after Father Christmas had departed. After the party, the carol singers would arrive from the village and were invited in for a glass of beer or cider, served by David from large barrels.

The children hung up their Christmas stockings until they were almost grown up and at 5.30 on Christmas morning the excitement became even more intense as they awoke to open them. They always contained an orange in the toe and envelopes containing money from the aunts and uncles. On one red-letter Christmas Pam found £5 in one of her envelopes.

After breakfast the family walked to Swinbrook church which was decorated with holly and chrysanthemums. Mr Foster always chose the children's favourite carols and preached a short sermon so that everyone could get home for Christmas lunch; after this a walk was deemed necessary to make way for the Christmas cake and then the event that Pam always dreaded – the dressing up.

The children vanished to the attic to choose their outfits from the dressing-up box, which was full of fancy-dress costumes and some of Sydney's old evening dresses. The costumes were supposed to be a secret but there were few surprises as everybody knew what was in the box. Nancy was the most inventive of the family but their father always wore the same dressing gown and a 'ghastly red wig'. Pam admitted that she was hopeless at dressing up and always went as Lady Rowena from Ivanhoe in a long red dress trimmed with orange beads. Debo still keeps those beads on her dressing table to remind her of Pam. The long dress meant that Pam could keep on her woolly knickers against the cold, but Nancy would never let her get away with it and would pull up her skirt to reveal her knee-length bloomers to the assembled party.

After supper the house party played a game called Commerce, for which David produced money prizes ranging from 10s to 1d. The Game often went on until 11.30 p.m., by which time the adults were visibly wilting while the children got more and more excited – the very young ones having been taken off to bed much earlier.

Boxing Day brought the gloomy thought that the guests would be going home the next day and life would return to normal. The children always longed for snow so that nobody could reach the station – a five-mile drive by pony and trap when the weather was too bad for the car. Pam remembered it happening only twice and felt that the adults may not have been as ecstatic as the children at finding their escape to London closed.

The excitement continued, however, for on New Year's Eve the mummers arrived and performed their traditional play with St George, the Dragon and the Turkish Knight, the village children reciting their parts in a monotone. It was in this group that a youthful Bob Arnold, who later played the part of Tom Forrest in *The Archers*, began his acting career.

All too soon it was Twelfth Night when the tree was dismantled and the decorations put away, as was the sponge and water bucket which David always hid behind the tree as a fire precaution, since Pam might not always be around to smell the smoke!

This amazing attention to detail and the obvious enjoyment with which it was related many years later is an example of how Pam carried the images in her head. She never lost her joy of Christmas; in fact, it probably increased in later years since she no longer had to endure the 'dreaded dressing up'.

Two

The Other Children

*D*avid and Sydney spent the first years of their married life in
London and it was here that the five eldest Mitford children
were born. They were brought up very much as other upper-
class children who lived in the capital, not seeing very much of their
parents and being in the care of a nanny when they were young and a
governess as they grew older. They went for walks in the park and were
sometimes allowed to visit the zoo or – oh joy! – Harrods pet shop
from which they acquired an assortment of animals, including rats, mice
and even a grass snake which Unity christened Enid. They played with
children of their own kind who lived nearby or with their many cousins.

As well as her convictions about the power of the Good Body to
heal itself, Sydney would not allow the children to eat pig meat, rabbit,
hare or shellfish, but David refused point blank to give up these tasty
meats which he had eaten all his life. This meant that the children
had the added agony of smelling the bacon, sausages, pigs' brains and
trotters which they were not allowed to eat unless one of the kitchen
staff secretly took pity on them. When Tom went to boarding school,
he wrote home triumphantly: 'We have sossidges every Sunday' – a
statement which no doubt provoked shrieks of envy among his sisters.

Both Sydney and David agreed on the subject of their children's education, the main thrust of which was that girls should be educated at home. David did not want daughters with thick calf muscles from playing hockey and Sydney was happy to teach the children herself and then engage a governess. Although Nancy and Jessica bemoaned the fact that they hadn't been allowed to go to school, they actually must have received a good education, particularly from their mother, who insisted that they should be able to read the leading article in *The Times* by the time they were 6. Later they were taught by Miss Mirams and Miss Hussey who came from the Charlotte Mason PNEU training college in Ambleside. They were taught French, as it was deemed to be a language that all well-bred young ladies should speak, and they were always encouraged to use the library which gave them a wealth of knowledge within easy reach. That their education was well up to standard is illustrated by the fact that when Tom went to his prep. school, he was put in a class for new boys who had got top marks in their entrance exam.

Some of the girls did, in fact, spend brief spells at school. In London Nancy went to the Frances Holland School close to the family home and later to Hatherop Castle School near Cirencester. Unity was sent twice to boarding school and twice asked to leave because of her disruptive behaviour, and Jessica, when the family was living at Asthall Manor, cycled to Burford School and persuaded the head-master to enrol her as a pupil. Sydney, however, wouldn't hear of her going because she might want to bring home children whom the family 'wouldn't know'. Such was life among the upper classes before the great changes in social mobility which began with the Great War. Diana and Debo felt ill at the thought of going to school and Pam was content just to be at home.

When the family was living in London, David worked as office manager at *The Lady*, a job given to him by his father-in-law, who had founded the magazine. It was not one which he relished, preferring to be outside, but he stuck at it in order to bring home an income to keep his ever-increasing family. Sydney also had a small income from her father but the Mitfords were not considered rich. However, because Sydney was such a good manager of money, she was able to afford to rent Old Mill Cottage in High Wycombe so that the children could be away from London during the heat of the summer. It was here that they had their first taste of country life which some grew to love and others to hate.

The outbreak of the First World War coincided with the birth of Unity, the Mitfords' fifth child and fourth daughter. This was something of a disappointment to David and Sydney who would have liked another boy, but they still felt there was plenty of time. Unity's second name was Valkyrie, the war maiden, and she was conceived in Swastika in Canada where David had a rather unproductive gold field. Both names were to prove prophetic. Despite having lost a lung while fighting in the Boer War, David managed to get to France where he became a dispatch rider, came under fire several times and was mentioned in dispatches.

Then the family received tragic news which was to change their lives for ever. David's elder brother Clement, much loved by everyone, was killed in May 1915, leaving a pregnant wife and a small daughter. David was so devastated that the thought of succeeding to the Redesdale title was far from his mind, but when Clement's widow produced another girl it became only a matter of time – since his father was already gravely ill – before he inherited the title and the vast Victorian house with five staircases which was Batsford Park. The expense of being in London with very little money during the war had meant that the young Mitford family was already living in a house on the Batsford estate, but in 1916 they moved into the mansion itself.

From the start it was obvious that the family could not afford to stay for long in a huge house where the upkeep was immense, but even David, who tended to sell when the market was low and buy again when it was high, realised that the war years were not a good time to put such a house on the market. The children always knew that they would not be there forever but they had a lot of fun playing hide and seek in the vast house, riding in the park with Hooper, hunting with the Heythrop hounds and being hunted themselves by their father's bloodhound.

The Child Hunt has been made much of by those seeking to equate David to Uncle Matthew in Nancy's semi-autobiographical novels *The Pursuit of Love* and *Love in a Cold Climate*, which have been dramatised – or in some instances over-dramatised – for television. In fact, the children loved being hunted and were not in the least frightened. They set off well ahead of David's pet bloodhound, laying as difficult a trail as possible, running through streams and among sheep and cattle to get rid of their scent. Then they would sit down and wait for the hound to find them. When he did he jumped all over them, licking them copiously until a breathless David arrived to call him off. He never pursued them on horseback – he had already given up riding after breaking his pelvis – and there was never a pack of hounds. In many ways he did resemble Uncle Matthew, but this was not one of them.

Much more tricky, now that most of the children were old enough to eat with their parents, was David's aversion to stickiness. He would fly into a rage if a child spilled food and the fact that no table napkins were allowed further added to the mealtime tension. While still in London, Sydney had decided that the laundering of the vast quantities of napkins used by the family was uneconomic; paper ones were not to be tolerated so none were used at all. Diana remembers the uneasiness when suet pudding was on the menu accompanied by Tate & Lyle's golden syrup. It was a great favourite with the children but if a single drop fell on the 'good tablecloth' there were bellows of rage from their father. In the end, one of the maids was given the task of serving the syrup which made for quieter mealtimes.

In 1917 yet another daughter was born to David and Sydney. She was called Jessica after Sydney's mother and yet again, although they would have liked another boy, she was a welcome addition to the ever-growing family. Sydney found it hard to make ends meet at Batsford and she began to keep bees and hens in order to make money to pay the salary of the redoubtable governess Miss Mirams, who also helped with the bees.

In 1919 Batsford was sold and the family moved to Asthall Manor, a very attractive Cotswold manor house not far from Burford in West Oxfordshire. It was David's intention eventually to build a house in

Swinbrook, the neighbouring village where he owned much of the land, and the family only stayed at Asthall for six years. They were, however, very formative years and the children loved the mellow stone house which looked out over the churchyard and where they could spend endless hours in the library which was in a separate building joined to the house by a covered way and with bedrooms above in which the older ones slept.

Since David owned the living of Swinbrook that was where the family went to church each Sunday, sitting in the family pew which David had had made from money he had won on the Grand National. The parson was only allowed to preach for ten minutes or David would start to look at his watch, but in spite of this the children were bored and the great sport among the girls was to make Tom 'blither' (i.e. laugh), at which they usually succeeded; they would also, bizarrely, lick the pew. Whatever did it taste of? Certainly not as nice as the sweets in the village shop in Swinbrook – toffee, acid drops, Edinburgh rock and butterscotch sold in squares of paper twisted into a bag by the village postmistress, who weighed out the sweets on the same brass scales which she used for the letters.

In 1920 at the age of 40, and in one last attempt to produce another son, Sydney had her seventh and last child – a girl, who was christened Deborah. In her book *Wait for Me*, Debo describes how there was no entry in her mother's engagement book for the day of her birth, 31 March. The first entry in April says in large letters, Kitchen Chimney Swept. She claims that, such was the disappointment, nobody except nanny looked at her for the first three months of her life. This neglect seems to have done her no lasting harm since of all the Mitford siblings, with the exception of Pam, she was the one who was the most balanced and the most happy with her lot, living in the countryside surrounded by a host of animals, seldom bored and always on good terms with her parents.

Boredom was something which frequently overcame Nancy, Diana, Jessica and Unity at various times of their lives and yet their lives were probably more interesting than those of many other young people of their time. They had a well-stocked library, they went on frequent trips to Oxford, and rather less frequent ones to the theatre at Stratford-upon-Avon, and they had visits from their many cousins and visited them in turn. All the family sang well and spent time singing round the piano which Sydney played. And then there were the animals. Where once the pets had been bought selectively from Harrods, now they had ponies, dogs and goats; Jessica had a sheep called Miranda to which she was devoted and they all kept hens and sold the eggs to make pocket money.

Something which few of them realised at the time was that they had particularly devoted parents. David's rages could not disguise the fact that he loved his children and, once they had moved to the country, played a big part in their childhood; while Sydney, though she often seemed distant and vague, lived for her family and was devastated by some of their later actions and by the deaths of Tom and then Unity. She was always there for her children, a fact which Nancy and Jessica found hard to accept but which Pam, Diana and Debo realised very early on in their lives.

Three

Growing Up

When Nancy once said that she thought sisters were a protection against life's cruel circumstances, Jessica replied that, as a child, her sisters *were* the cruel circumstances. Nancy was certainly Pam's main cruel circumstance since she teased her unmercifully through childhood and beyond, still harbouring the jealousy that had overwhelmed her when Pam was born.

While some of the teasing was surely intended for fun, much of it was undoubtedly cruel. For instance, when Nancy and Pam were debutantes Nancy would find out the name of the boy that Pam was keen on and tell her she had seen him out with another girl. Pam, as always, bore her sister no malice but it must have made her miserable at the time.

Nancy was capable of making all her sisters laugh with harmless – or relatively harmless – teases. Her skill at dressing up was unsurpassed in the family. One of Pam's favourite stories was of the Christmas when Nancy was nowhere to be seen as everyone else gathered in their costumes and guests sat down to dinner. Finally, as they were leaving the dining room, the hinged window seat slowly creaked open to reveal the missing sister 'dressed' as an Egyptian mummy.

Another tease much laughed about in the family happened during the General Strike of 1926 when Pam and Nancy helped to run a temporary canteen for strike-breaking lorry drivers. This was while they were living at Asthall Manor and the canteen was in a barn not far away, on the main road between Burford and Oxford. Pam was an early riser so she took the early shift. She was also the only one who knew how to make tea and sandwiches and wash up. In any case, Nancy moaned about having to do more than hand out the sandwiches. 'Oh, darling, you know how much I hate taking things out of ovens, one's poor hands … besides, I do so loathe getting up early.' Although the canteen fare did not involve ovens at all, Pam was still happy to oblige. Even then she showed the gift for catering which remained with her for the rest of her life, and to which her sisters never aspired.

At five o'clock one morning Pam was alone at the canteen and, getting somewhat impatient because there were no customers, she lay on the ground with her ear to the road in the hope of hearing an approaching lorry. She had just gone back to her post in front of the tea and sandwiches when a disgusting tramp lurched towards her and asked for a cup of tea. While she was pouring it, he came round the counter, put a filthy arm around her waist and thrust his horribly scarred face into hers, demanding a kiss. Pam shrieked and ran, but fell over and badly twisted her ankle in her attempt at flight. The tramp, of course, was Nancy. Pam, being Pam, laughed as much as the others, in spite of her injury.

Indeed, Pam was by far the most contented of all the sisters. She was the only one, except Debo, who genuinely loved country life and was never bored by her rural existence. Although academically she lagged well behind Nancy, she had a sharp sense of business, most likely inherited from her mother. This began at an early age when all the children rented small plots of land from their father on which to raise their various animals. Pam insisted that she should be invited to the dinner which David gave for tenant farmers and, although he tried to refuse, he had to relent because she was also a tenant.

At the dinner, the farmer sitting next to her asked her what rent she paid and she discovered that, size for size, she was paying about twice as much as he was. At his suggestion she asked her father for a reduction and although he was reluctant to do this, her point was a valid one and her rent was reduced. Of all the sisters, Pam was the one who was never out of favour with her often volatile father, perhaps because they shared an enduring love of the countryside and country pursuits.

It was Pam and later Debo who were particularly skilled at animal husbandry, but all the sisters loved living creatures and were very soft-hearted towards them. Hens were a particular favourite and, like their mother, they managed to make some money by selling eggs. Later, Nancy famously kept a hen in her Paris flat and the nicknames of Hen and Henderson, which Jessica and Debo gave to one another, refer to their obsession with poultry. Likewise, the Hons Cupboard at Swinbrook House, where all the children would congregate to keep warm, and Jessica's best-selling account of the Mitford family, *Hons and Rebels*, were not so called because they were all honourables – hon stood for hen in their special language.

Pam's sense of the value of things, as shown from her argument with her father over her rent, stayed with her all her life, some of the tales of her 'carefulness' causing howls of laughter among the other sisters. But this did not mean she was ungenerous. For instance, when Diana had her appendix removed, everybody made a great fuss of her, especially Pam, aged 10, who bought her a magnificent paint box. Diana's appendectomy was a dramatic tale often related by the sisters, particularly Pam whose memory always served her so well: the operation was performed by the local doctor on the kitchen table at Batsford from where the patient was removed to one of the comfortable guest rooms to convalesce. Presumably, Sydney realised that this was another occasion when the Good Body would not recover on its own.

When Nancy finally achieved her dream of going to Hatherop Castle, a boarding school near Cirencester for local upper-class girls, Pam and

Diana were taken there once a week for dancing lessons so that they would not disgrace themselves when they became debutantes. Still somewhat lame from her childhood illness, Pam never shone at these classes but they were much enjoyed by all three sisters, in spite of the fact that the two younger ones had travelled from Asthall to Hatherop, a distance of at least 15 miles, in the outside dickey seat of their father's Morris Cowley. In winter, despite being covered up with David's old trench coats, they arrived shivering with cold and with the prospect of travelling home the same way in the freezing darkness. Pam, who felt the cold all her life (her thick cardigans were legendary), must have dreaded these journeys but, true to form, she never grumbled and neither she nor Diana had any desire to join Nancy permanently at school.

Another spin-off (though not a welcome one) for Pam and Diana of Nancy's time at Hatherop Castle was that Nancy became a Girl Guide; when she returned home she persuaded their mother to let her form a Swinbrook troop of which she would be captain, with her two younger sisters as her patrol leaders and troop members recruited from the village girls. Sydney thought it an excellent idea and Pam good-naturedly fell in with Nancy's plans, but Diana hated every minute of it which further pleased Nancy as it was yet another tease to discomfort her sister.

Diana described guiding to be 'all I had feared and more. Ten of the village girls were told they had to join and Pam and I picked sides for our patrols.' Even worse was the uniform – stiff blue drill dresses, black stockings and shoes, and hard, round felt hats; to add insult to injury, Nancy had a different and rather becoming hat turned up at one side with a cockade. 'We stumped about at the end of the garden, trying to light damp things with three matches and run a hundred yards in twenty seconds.' They held competitions to see who could collect the most useful things (with Sydney as judge) and learnt first-aid techniques with bandages and tourniquets. Her mother had promised Diana that she could give it up at the end of the year if she still hated it, but she reneged on her promise as 'it was doing the village girls so much good'. Eventually Nancy grew tired of it, much to Diana's relief, and probably Pam's too, though she never complained.

Pam was quite happy to put up with most of the guiding activities
but what annoyed even her was Nancy's ability to make a successful
bonfire out of twigs and damp leaves. Every year the children had a
bonfire to clear up their gardening plots for the winter. Nancy's was
next to Pam's and Diana's, and while the two younger girls desperately tried to get their barely smoking heaps to catch light by means
of adding more newspaper, Nancy's fire would be blazing away and
Nancy would crouch in front of it 'like a triumphant witch', singing
'Burning, burning, merrily burning' in the accent of the Czechish
lady doctor. Pam must have learned a lesson or two from Nancy
because in later life, in her Gloucestershire kitchen garden, she could
light a bonfire which burned very merrily, with the help of Gerald
Stewart, her faithful gardener for many years.

Nancy paved the way for many of the others' activities and one of
these was a trip to Paris in the year before she became a debutante.
Nancy adored Paris and was to live there in later life, referred to by
her sisters as the French Lady Writer or simply Lady. After that each
of the girls went to Paris before coming out. Nancy and Diana certainly lived it up there, but Pam's Paris trip, as might be expected, was
incident free. It was 1923 and she obviously enjoyed herself because
the letters she wrote to her mother are full of details of the balls she
had been invited to and the clothes she would wear to them. She was
particularly excited by the thought of a fancy-dress party, to which
her group of girlfriends had decided to dress as Arab women so that
the boys would not know which was which – not perhaps something
which would be considered politically correct today – but it did show
that she had got over her childhood horror of dressing up.

Typically, though, the greatest excitement was a ride in a tank. 'I
should love to do the whole thing over again. I hardly think I have
ever enjoyed anything so much.' Quiet Pam, of all the sisters, probably
had the greatest sense of adventure. 'She was very courageous and
she inherited this courage from our mother,' her sister Debo told me
many years later.

Pam's coming-out dance in 1924 was actually in fancy dress and
Pam went as Madame de Pompadour, whose biography Nancy was

to write in later life. 'I felt very self-conscious because I was rather fat,' she said later, confessing that she didn't enjoy any of the coming-out dances but wrote in her diary that she had had a marvellous time because she didn't in the future want to be considered a failure at parties. Diana, the kindest sister, blamed this lack of self-confidence on Nancy's spiteful teasing, but in a strange way the teasing made Pam the very individual and extraordinarily attractive woman she became in later years. In those days, too, she was considered a beauty, with her bright blue eyes and naturally streaked blonde hair, an effect which many girls today pay their hairdressers large sums of money to achieve.

At that time – the roaring twenties – hair was a pressing problem for Pam and Diana who needed their parents' permission to have their hair bobbed like Nancy. The Redesdales were very strict when it came to appearance and the girls were not allowed to wear basic make-up as their contemporaries did. Even 8-year-old Debo was recruited to write to their mother, who was in Canada at the time, to beg that the two sisters be allowed to have short hair.

Pam still loved the more simple family traditions which she had enjoyed in childhood. One of these was Bailey Week which took place at the home of their cousins, Richard, Anthony, Christopher and Timothy Bailey; these were the sons of Aunt Weenie, Sydney's youngest sister, who had married Colonel Percy Bailey and lived at nearby Stow-on-the-Wold. Activities included cricket, tennis, walks, riding, picnics and dancing, and all the girls looked forward to it immensely. Even in the full activity of her London debutante season, Pam wrote to her mother to say how much she was looking forward to Bailey Week. In fact, it was probably a welcome relief from all those balls that she had to pretend she enjoyed.

Thus shy Pam began adult life. It was on the surface a life less action-packed than those of her sisters, but, as the years went by, they began to see that she, who had long been the butt of jokes, who seldom stuck her head above the parapet for fear of more teasing, was the one on whom they came to depend. Of all the sisters, she was the one to whom the family and its origins probably meant most of all and it is not insignificant that she was the only one who read – and she found reading a slow process – her grandfather Redesdale's account of the time he spent in the Far East. Entitled *Tales of Old Japan*, it remained in a prominent position on her bookshelves all her life. She also ploughed through two fat volumes of Bartie's *Memories* which Jessica found 'monstrously boring'.

Four

Teenage Sisters

In a family the size of the Mitfords, growing up was a long-drawn-out process. There was a sixteen-year gap between the eldest and the youngest and Sydney made Nancy one of Debo's godmothers, fearing that she might not live long enough to see her grow up. In fact, Nancy survived her mother, who lived to be 83, by only ten years.

It says a great deal for Sydney's stamina and her determination to launch her daughters into a world where they would find suitable husbands (the only option open to girls of their class and generation, although times were changing fast) that she endured six dreary debutante seasons, sitting at dances night after night when she must have longed to go to bed. It meant spending the summers in London when she must have hankered after her West Oxfordshire garden and she probably never knew that often, when a dance was particularly boring, the girls would leave by a back entrance and go to a nightclub, returning at a time when they felt they might be expected.

Nancy was obviously the first to be presented at court but, having taken this big step towards adulthood, found it somewhat unfulfilling; she was therefore determined to surround herself with a set of interesting friends, mostly Oxford undergraduates, who, if they were brave enough, accepted invitations to dine or even stay at Asthall and later Swinbrook. David hated having people other than family members in the house and many of these friends, known as the aesthetes, were bawled out if they did something to offend him – which wasn't difficult. Like Uncle Matthew in *The Pursuit of Love*, he really did call them 'sewers', though this was derived from a Tamil word which he had learned in Ceylon. Sua meant pig and it was difficult to know which was the greater insult. Even worse was his habit of calling down the table to Sydney at the end of dinner: 'Have these people no homes of their own?' Relations between David and his favourite daughter were, unsurprisingly, very strained at this time.

Nancy had also developed a delight in foreign travel, first fostered during a visit to Europe when she was 17. She went on a school trip with a friend and the group visited France and Italy. Nancy was enthralled, finding each city more beautiful than the last – life seemed very boring when she returned to Asthall and she could not then see her way to making her home 'abroad'. She was, however, allowed to return to Paris in order to learn to speak French more fluently than in the schoolroom.

This was the roaring twenties and there was a lot of fun to be had at home. During her coming-out season and then at hunt balls and house parties Nancy danced and larked with the young post-war generation, who were called the Bright Young Things, a phrase taken up by Evelyn Waugh who became a close friend of Nancy. Her only complaint was that her clothes were not as fashionable as those of her fellow debutantes. They were home-made and she felt that they looked it. Although she had a small allowance from her parents, it did not go far into paying for the lifestyle to which she aspired. Her passion for 'abroad' and for stylish clothes were not fulfilled until her novels brought in enough income for a Paris flat and couture by Dior.

Diana was becoming increasingly bored at home but this boredom was soon to be relieved by a trip to Paris where Sydney took the girls in the autumn of 1926, mainly to settle Diana into a day school where she could be 'finished' and also improve her French. The family stayed in a modest hotel close to the home of Sydney's friends the Helleus. Monsieur Helleu was an artist and he became obsessed with Diana's beauty, painting her often and becoming a close friend. The family returned home for Christmas but afterwards Diana was allowed to go back to Paris and live in a boarding house while she completed her year at school. She travelled as far as Paris with her cousins Winston Churchill and his son Randolph, who were on their way to Italy to meet Mussolini.

Nancy and Pam had already lived in Paris so Diana was not short of friends and she made the most of her new-found freedom. Her great sorrow was that M. Helleu died during this time. He had been a faithful admirer and she mourned for him, but it didn't stop her having a good time in a city where it was not compulsory to be chaperoned everywhere she went.

Keeping a diary of her activities, however, proved her undoing. When she returned home for the Easter holidays she made the mistake of leaving her diary open in the sitting room while she went out for a walk. Sydney read the entry which described a visit to the cinema alone with a young man one afternoon in Paris. This was an unforgivable crime and Diana was forbidden to return to school and condemned to spend the summer with the younger children in Devon. It was a terrible punishment and because she was bored, literally to tears, this must have contributed greatly to Diana's determination to get away from the family home.

By the late summer of 1927 the family home was no longer their beloved Asthall, but Swinbrook, which was entirely built to David's design with Sydney, mysteriously, since she had excellent taste and was a superb homemaker, playing no part. Instead of nestling in a village it was perched on top of a hill and was draughty and uncomfortable. The children each had a bedroom of their own in which was a small fireplace, but they were not allowed a fire. The only warm place was the enormous linen cupboard with its distinctive smell of airing clothes, immortalised as the Hons Cupboard in Nancy's *The Pursuit of Love*. It was here that the younger children, Unity, Decca (Jessica) and Debo, gathered to hatch schemes, work out the rules for

their new Hons Society or talk to one another in one of their special languages, Boudledidge spoken by Unity and Decca, or Honnish
which was the secret means of communication between Decca and
Debo. What the older children especially missed was the large library
at Asthall, set apart from the house, with their bedrooms above which
they had made especially their own. But family life was changing fast
and it would not be long before Nancy, Pam and Diana were leaving
home for good. Tom was already studying in Vienna and in the end
it was only Debo who really regarded Swinbrook as home and was
happy there.

Eventually, David and Sydney relented towards Diana and in
the autumn she was allowed to stay with the Churchill family at
Chartwell, their country home. Here she met some very interesting people, including top-grade scientist Professor Lindemann, who
became Churchill's chief scientific advisor during the next war.
Lindemann suggested that she might learn German and as Tom was
studying German in Vienna, she asked her parents if she might do so
too. Needless to say, after the Paris debacle, they refused point blank.

The following year, 1928, was Diana's debutante season and within
weeks she had met and fallen in love with Bryan Guinness. Boredom
over, she eventually overcame her parents' opposition on account of
their age – she was 18 and he was 22 when they met – and they were
married at St Margaret's church, Westminster, the following year, on
29 January 1929. It was the 'society wedding of the year' but it was
somewhat marred for Diana by the fact that Decca and Debo, who
had looked forward to the event with wild excitement, went down
with an unidentified infectious disease and could not be bridesmaids.
It was left to 14-year-old Unity, who was very self-conscious about
her height and her straight, sticking-out fair hair and who definitely
did not want to be a bridesmaid, to represent the family.

Following Diana's engagement to Bryan, Pam became engaged to
Oliver Watney, a member of another brewing family. Nancy, obviously
not wanting to be the elder sister 'left on the shelf', announced that
she was unofficially engaged to Hamish St Clair-Erskine, who was
four years younger and unsuitable in many ways, not least because he

was homosexual, a fact which Nancy seemed unaware of or simply did not want to admit. Sydney and David were against it, as was Tom, who had had a brief affair with Hamish at Eton before deciding that he preferred women. But Hamish was intensely amusing and to be amused was what Nancy loved best. The 'engagement' dragged on for four years but eventually came to nothing.

In 1928 Nancy persuaded her parents to let her attend the Slade School of Art but she lasted there only a month, being told by the director of the school that she had no talent. This upset her greatly and she began to write short gossip pieces instead for glossy magazines such as *Vogue* and *Harper's Bazaar*. She then talked herself into a job with the family magazine, *The Lady*, and not long afterwards her first novel, *Highland Fling*, was published. The Lady Writer was on her way.

Unity was shy and sensitive as a small child. When something which upset her was said at mealtimes she would slide under the table and not come out until she felt like doing so. This was understood and no one took any notice. She also had a strange diet for some time, eating nothing but mashed potatoes. However, a liking for strawberries at the age of 6 got her into real trouble. She and her cousin Christopher Bailey, also given to mischief, once ate all the strawberries in the greenhouse, which were being kept for a special occasion. This was one of the stories, much related, which became part of Mitford family history.

Unity drew well and could memorise reams of poetry by heart, but as she grew up she became very boisterous and had a habit of picking up Miss Dell, one of the many governesses, who was very small, and putting her on the sideboard. As Miss Dell also taught the children the art of shoplifting, she didn't last long, and Miss Hussey, her successor, was constantly sending Unity to confess her antics to her mother. Miss Hussey suggested that boarding school might be a good idea but in the end it was Unity's constant nagging that persuaded David and Sydney to send her to St Margaret's School, Bushey, in January 1929. Although she could be moody and wilful, her parents had little trouble with her as a child and she was loved in the family for her hilarity and sense of humour. In a family of individuals, she was possibly the most eccentric, but this eccentricity did not go down well at St Margaret's and she was eventually asked to leave, though, according to Sydney, she was heartbroken and always remembered the school with affection.

Her behaviour continued to be somewhat disruptive, however, and legend has it that she took great delight during her debutante season in letting loose her pet rat, Ratular, at coming-out dances and once even at Buckingham Palace. Enid, her grass snake, possibly also made the odd appearance at debutante dances, to the general alarm of the other guests and to Unity's glee.

After Diana married, Jessica, for whom she had always been the favourite sister, missed her badly and it was possibly from this time that her extreme rebelliousness and dissatisfaction with life began. As a young child she is remembered as being pretty, very funny and happy with her lot. Like the others she loved her animals, especially her pet sheep Miranda who became her constant companion. But unlike the others during childhood, she was far from being an outdoor girl, much preferring reading to riding. Diana spent hours with her in the pony paddock trying to teach her to ride her pony Joey, coaxing her to climb back onto him when she fell off for the umpteenth time.

Unity being sent to boarding school and Jessica not being allowed to go to school in Burford were probably other turning points; they transformed her from the little girl who would take hold of her father's arm and shake it, telling him that she was giving him 'palsy practice' for his old age, into a bored and resentful teenager who couldn't wait to leave home. She opened an account at Drummond's Bank in which to save her 'running away money' – mainly her pocket money and the Christmas presents she received from various aunts. In the family the account was regarded as a joke and Nancy used it in *The Pursuit of Love*, where Linda's little sister Jassy also has a running away fund, but Jessica was deadly serious as later events were to show. Tom, when he came home, realised that Jessica's main problem was boredom with her situation and, ever the bookworm himself, introduced her to the sort of writers he felt she would enjoy. This helped but did not solve the problem.

Despite the differences in their outlook, Jessica and Debo were close companions. They would talk all day in Honnish, which was less incomprehensible than Boudledidge, being largely 'normal' English spoken with a Gloucestershire accent, and they shared each other's secrets. But this close relationship was severely put to the test when Unity went to St Margaret's and Jessica became moody and critical about everything to do with the family.

Debo found this attitude hard to understand because she was so happy with her life at Swinbrook, surrounded by a host of animals and on good terms with both her parents. David and Sydney were probably more indulgent to her partly because she was the youngest and also because she enjoyed the same things as they did: going fishing and shooting with her father and tending her poultry with the same care as Sydney. The thought of going to boarding school made her, like Diana, feel physically sick, but ironically, when Jessica, aged 16, went to study French in Paris as the older sisters had done, it was deemed to be cheaper to send Debo to boarding school than have a governess for an only child.

The school was in Oxford; Debo described it as smelling of lino, girls and fish and she hated it – so much so that she fainted in a geometry lesson and was sick several times. She persuaded Sydney to let her leave but the term's fees had been paid in advance. They compromised: Debo went back as a day girl for the rest of the term and after that was taught, with Celia Hay, one of Sydney's friend's children, by the kindly Miss Frost.

Hunting was one of Debo's great delights, as it had been Nancy's, but she also loved skating and was very good at it, as were David and Sydney. On Saturdays she went hunting and on Sundays David and his younger brother Jack took her skating in Oxford. She had already learned to skate on a family holiday in Pontresina and the regular visits to the Oxford rink made her good enough to be 'spotted' by a trainer who suggested to Sydney that Debo could potentially make the British junior team. Sydney rejected the idea and Debo did not find out about it until later in life and was sorry that she had not had the chance to excel at something she loved. But unlike the others –

except, of course, for Pam – she did not harbour resentment against her mother, either then or at any time.

Rather like Pam, Tom tends to be somewhat neglected in the history of the Mitford family, probably because, in the words of one of the children's nannies, he was 'no trouble'. But he was still very much his own man in this largely female family. Loved by his parents and his sisters, he did well at prep. school, at Eton and then in Vienna, where he studied music and learnt to speak German better than any other member of the family. He was a gifted musician and could easily have taken it up as a career. In the event he chose law and became a respected barrister.

David, never an intellectual himself, was somewhat in awe of Tom's knowledge, shown by the fact that he asked him to organise the Asthall library at the tender age of 10. His teachers respected him and he had lots of good friends. Many people would have been spoiled by all this affection and regard but it seems never to have gone to Tom's head. Possibly the rough and tumble in a family of teasing, noisy sisters had discouraged him from having the high opinion of himself that his many gifts deserved. He was the first of the family to feel the fascination of a re-emerging Germany and he lived for some time not in Germany, but in Austria, in a castle belonging to a Hungarian, Janos von Almasy, who became a lifelong friend of Tom's, and later Unity's. It was often rumoured that Janos would have liked to marry Pam – John Betjeman certainly regarded him as a rival.

By the end of a turbulent decade, in which the country had now entered a period of severe financial depression, the Mitford children had begun to leave the nest. Nancy, although she still lived at home for periods, had embarked on her writing career; Diana was married with one small son and another on the way; and Pam was managing Bryan and Diana's farm at Biddesden in Hampshire. Unity and Jessica were beginning to form the extreme and opposing views which would eventually separate them forever and Debo was living the kind of life she would always enjoy. As yet the political extremes which were to divide the family were only starting to smoulder. It would not be long before they caused violent eruptions.

Five

Out into the World

Pam's engagement to Oliver Watney did not last long. Togo, as he was known, was a tall, dark, stooping young man who suffered from chronic tuberculosis, for which there was then no cure. He lived at Cornbury, not far from Swinbrook, and probably only proposed to Pam because his father was keen on the match, which would have had the advantage of uniting an older, aristocratic family with the Watney commercial interests.

Before this, in a letter to Diana, who was at Bexhill recuperating after having her tonsils out, Pam had confessed to feeling intensely shy at the prospect of being left on her own with Togo, an event which she knew some of her friends were planning:

> I do so wish you were here. You see I feel so stupid because everyone invited Togo to tea on Sunday to play tennis and everyone is to fade away and leave us two together! If you were here you would of course join in and I should not feel so young. However, I shall have to get over feeling shy and this weekend is sure to help me in doing so. I should really much prefer to be in Bexhill with you.

Hardly the words of a young woman in love.

When Togo's father died of a heart attack his mother made it her business to talk him out of his engagement to Pam. His heart was obviously not entirely given to Pam because he seems to have succumbed to his mother without much opposition. Possibly the prospect of those five sharp-witted, shrieking sisters sapped his already waning enthusiasm. He was sent on a cruise for his health and on his return went to see Pam to break off the engagement.

The family was outraged by Togo's treachery and Nancy wrote Pam a sympathetic letter of the sort that she had probably never written to her before:

> Oh I am so sorry how beastly for you poor darling. Never mind I expect you'll be rewarded by marrying someone millions of times nicer & obviously Togo would have been a horrid husband. Are you going to Canada? I do hope so, that would be lovely for you.
> Best love and don't be too miserable, I am, dreadfully, but one must make the best of things.
> Heaps of love, Naunce

Pam, though initially very disappointed that the engagement was off, was relieved because she realised she was not in love with him. She was eventually to meet someone with whom Togo could not have ever hoped to compete. The wedding presents had to be returned and most of this somewhat embarrassing task was done by Tom who drove round London in his little car. A notice appeared in *The Times* announcing that the marriage would not now take place.

The Togo saga was not quite over, however. The engagement ring which he had given Pam was a replica of King Alfred's jewel, the original of which was in the Ashmolean Museum in Oxford. True to form, Nancy said that it looked like a chicken's mess which upset Pam, in spite of her lifelong love of chickens. Nancy saved up the incident to use in *The Pursuit of Love*.

Linda, whose disagreeableness at this time knew no bounds, said that it [the engagement ring of her sister Louisa] looked like a chicken's mess. Same shape, same size, same colour. 'Not my idea of a jewel.'

'I think it's lovely,' said Aunt Sadie, but Linda's words had left their sting all the same.

Long afterwards, when Pam was asked what had become of the chicken's mess, she replied that she had given it to Unity. 'And what did Unity do with it?' 'Oh, she gave it to Hitler.' How many jilted fiancées could say that?

When the necessary wedding arrangements had been cancelled Pam went with her parents to spend the summer prospecting for gold in Canada. In 1912 David had laid claim to 40 acres of a new goldfield in northern Ontario. Although today this seems like foolish speculation, there was actually gold to be found in the vicinity and the Mitfords' neighbour, Sir Harry Oakes, had made millions from prospecting, before being murdered in the Bahamas.

Very little gold, however, was found on the Mitfords' patch but some happy holidays were enjoyed there. David and Sydney went out for the first time in 1913. They lived in a log cabin and Sydney – who had learnt domestic skills aboard her father's boat, on which she had spent much of her childhood – did the cooking and cleaning. In her unpublished biography of Unity, Sydney makes it clear that it was here that Unity was conceived. By a strange quirk of fate, in the light of future events, the place was called Swastika which, even more ironically, is derived from a Sanskrit word meaning 'a feeling of well being'.

Although, as always, gold was only found in small quantities in the summer of 1928, Pam was in her element at Swastika since she, too, could indulge in her domestic skills and live in the simple way she loved. Possibly also she enjoyed a little respite from her siblings. She and her parents lived in what the family called 'the shack' – a substantial log cabin where there were no servants and where Pam and her mother did the housework, cooked and pumped water by hand. Sydney made bread to her own special recipe, which she did for the rest of her life. Baked with stone-ground wholemeal flour and deliciously crusty, it is now immortalised on the internet (look up Lady Redesdale's Bread) and Pam baked loaves to her mother's recipe right into old age. For Pam, the gold-mining period must have been a source of great delight for she always kept a framed photograph of her father at Swastika in her home.

During the time Pam was there Jessica wrote to say that Nancy was sharing a house in London with the soon-to-be-famous novelist Evelyn Waugh and his new wife, the former Evelyn Gardener (the pair were known to their friends as he-Evelyn and she-Evelyn). They would be doing all their own housework, just like Pam and their mother in Canada.

Perhaps luckily for Nancy, who never aspired to domesticity of any kind (Pam's womanly gifts were always a source of 'wondair' to the other sisters), the arrangement with the Waughs did not last long. She-Evelyn left her husband a month later and the threesome went their separate ways. But the friendship between Nancy and Waugh survived, with a few inevitable hiccoughs, for the rest of their lives.

In 1930 Bryan and Diana bought a 350-acre farm and a herd of fifty cows at Biddesden in Hampshire, and Pam offered to manage it for them and to run the milk round. It was the start of a very happy time for Pam who had acquired enough farming knowledge to make her position viable. In the end she stayed there for four years, longer than Diana herself who eventually left Bryan for Sir Oswald Mosley.

With her blonde hair and blue eyes, and wearing breeches and boots alongside the farm workers, Pam caused quite a stir among the traditional old farmers at Andover market where she went to buy stock. She grew to be a successful bidder for good animals but early on she made a mistake which became one of the many, many jokes in the Mitford family annals. Having bought what she thought was a very good cow, when she got it back to Biddesden she discovered that 'the brute was bagless'. Nancy couldn't resist using this incident in her third published novel, *Wigs on the Green*. Even so, Pam made a reasonably good job of farming, even at a very poor time for agriculture. The farm workers, who called her 'Miss Pam', had a healthy respect for her, mainly because she showed them that she was not afraid of hard physical work.

Pam's farming experience stood her in good stead for when she kept cattle at Rignell Hall after her marriage and during the war. One of the stories much related in the family was of the bitterly cold winter of 1942 when all the water tanks for the cattle froze solid. The lad who had replaced her cowman (who had joined the armed forces) told her that there was no need to fetch fresh water for the cows because they could eat the snow. But Pam had heard that one before. 'How do you know what they want? You've never been an in-calf heifer,' she admonished the hapless boy.

During her time at Biddesden Pam met many of the Guinness's friends, and although she lived in a small house in the grounds, she often dined with Bryan and Diana and their many guests from the worlds of politics, the arts and science. One night she met the youthful John Betjeman, and other guests included artist Augustus John, writer Lytton Strachey and his mistress Dora Carrington, eminent scientist Professor Lindemann and the Sitwell and Huxley families. A very frequent guest was Randolph Churchill, the Mitfords' cousin, who became godfather, together with Evelyn Waugh, to Diana and Bryan's eldest son, Jonathan.

John Betjeman had been a friend of Bryan's since their Oxford days when they were successful editors of the university magazine *Cherwell*. He was on the rebound from an unsuccessful love affair but when he met Pam at Biddesden he fell in love with her. She had formed no romantic attachment since the Togo debacle and the two spent a lot of time in one another's company.

Betjeman at that time was mad on kite-flying and always arrived with a kite to fly with Pam. They would also drive round Wiltshire and Hampshire looking at churches and picnicking in the glorious countryside. On Sundays they cycled to the old church at nearby Appleshaw for matins, both enjoying the traditional liturgy and hymns. In these outings with 'Miss Pam', as he called her, it is possible to see the beginning of the interest in churches and church liturgy which remained with Betjeman for the rest of his life.

Since riding was the sport which all the sisters (except Jessica) adored, Pam decided to teach her latest admirer to ride. She put him on an old pony and sent him off into the woods behind the house where she thought he would be safe. But the local hunt was abroad and the sound of the horn was too much even for this 'bombproof' old mount, who ditched the future poet laureate and galloped off to look for foxes.

Betjeman was reluctant to make any obvious advances, partly because he had heard of Pam's attraction to a friend of Tom's, an Austrian aristocrat named Janos von Almasy, referred to by his English rival as 'that ghastly Czecheslovakian count'. Diana, however, was very much in favour of Betjeman and he continued his frequent visits to Biddesden where many a night was whiled away by Bryan doing conjuring tricks after dinner and the guests singing round the piano.

Betjeman proposed twice to Pam and the first time she turned him down without hesitation. On the second occasion he asked her to take some time to think about it. Before she could refuse again a tragedy occurred at Biddesden. Two weeks after Lytton Strachey's death from cancer, Dora Carrington shot herself on the estate with a gun she had borrowed from Bryan. After things had quietened down, and still with no definite reply from Pam, Betjeman wrote semi-jokingly to Nancy: 'If Pamela Mitford refuses me finally, you might marry me – I'm rich, handsome and aristocratic.' It is interesting to speculate how playing second fiddle, even in jest, to the sister of whom she had always been particularly jealous, went down with Nancy.

Many years later Pam told Betjeman's daughter, Candida Lycett Green: 'Betj made me laugh. I was very, very fond of him, but I wasn't in love with him. He said he'd like to marry me but I rather declined.' But they remained very good friends and when Betjeman was old and ill and many of his friends had stopped visiting him, he could always rely on a visit from kind Pam, the Rural Mitford, as he liked to call her.

It was Betjeman, too, who first coined the now well-known phrase which collectively describes the sisters when he wrote a little poem 'in honour of the Mitford Girls, but especially in honour of Miss Pamela':

The Mitford Girls! The Mitford Girls
I love them for their sins

The young ones all like 'Cavalcade,'
The old like 'Maskelyns'
SOPHISTICATION, Blessed dame
Sure they have heard her call
Yes, even Gentle Pamela
Most rural of them all.

It was even rumoured at one time that Betjeman's celebrated tennis girl, Miss Joan Hunter Dunn, the subject of his poem 'Pot Pourri in a Surrey Garden', whose identity had caused speculation for many years, was actually Pam. 'Oh, no,' she declared when I asked her. 'It couldn't have been me. I was *hopeless* at tennis.'

After leaving Biddesden in the mid-1930s, Pam became an intrepid and adventurous traveller, driving round Europe in her little Morris car. 'I called it the Stork because I had it specially painted grey with red wheels,' she said. Several of the countries she visited were absorbed behind the Iron Curtain after the Second World War and she must have been one of the last people to see them as they once were.

One such trip, which she related to me many years later, was to the foothills of the Carpathian Mountains. While in Vienna she had met a young man who needed to get to a shooting party in that region.

I offered to take him because I thought that the Carpathians were just beyond the Dolomites, but in fact it was a two-day drive along unmade roads. While it was dry we couldn't see for the dust and when it rained the water poured down the roads in torrents. But the greatest hazard was the horses. None of them had ever seen a car before – we didn't see any either, during the whole journey – so they were very frightened by the sight. We had the choice of whizzing past and getting the 'danger' over quickly or stopping and letting them pass. But whatever we did they took fright and dumped their drivers in the ditch.

Finally, the faithful Stork got them to their destination, whereupon their hostess expressed her pleasure that they had had a safe journey

A Subaltern's Love Song

and her surprise that they hadn't had a puncture. 'And that is just as well as I see you only have one spare tyre. In Czechoslovakia we always carry three.' But Pam had no intention of having British customs criticised, however well meant that criticism might be. 'Ah, but I bet your tyres aren't Dunlops,' she replied, with a sharpness which would have done credit to any of her sisters.

On her second visit to Germany in 1935 Unity introduced Pam to Hitler. The two girls had just finished eating lunch at the Osteria Bavaria in Munich, where Unity had previously hung about for hours hoping for a glimpse of the Führer before eventually being invited to his table. Suddenly there was a flurry of activity and Hitler and his henchmen arrived. Unity sent Pam to stand by the door in order to get a good look at him and he immediately spotted the tall, blonde young woman whose eyes were an even brighter blue than Unity's. He surmised that she was Unity's sister and the two were invited to eat a second lunch, which they happily did.

Pam was not impressed by Hitler, describing him on her return to England as 'very ordinary, like an old farmer in his brown suit'. Nevertheless, she remembered the meal they had eaten in every detail, especially the delicious new potatoes. In this she more than lived up to her sisters' boast that she could recall every detail of every meal she had ever eaten.

She also took no notice of Hitler's warning, when he heard of her motoring exploits, that 'it is very dangerous for a young woman to travel around Europe without a chaperone'. It was lucky that she disregarded him because she was fortunate enough to see some of the most beautiful European countries and their traditions before he brought about their ruin.

Unlike Diana, Unity and Jessica, Pam's political leanings were not a subject for much discussion. Fascism certainly did not appeal and although she always got on well with Sir Oswald Mosley, she never shared his, Diana's nor Unity's political opinions. Nor did Jessica's extreme left-wing views hold any attraction for her.

Life for Pam, however, was about to change in a big way, for in 1936 she met and married a most remarkable man.

Six

Derek

*D*avid, Lord Redesdale, is reputed to have referred to three of his sons-in-law as 'the man Mosley', 'the boy Romilly' (the cousin of Churchill with whom Jessica ran away when they were both 19) and 'the bore Rodd'. Peter Rodd was the husband of Nancy but the marriage did not last. He does not, however, seem to have found an adjective to describe Derek Jackson, whom Pam married at the end of 1936. This is hardly surprising since there was no category into which Derek fitted. He was truly a man of many parts.

Derek Jackson and his brother Vivian were the twin sons of Sir Charles Jackson, a Welshman who was by turns an architect, barrister and an expert on antique silver. He was also one of the founders of the *News of the World* whose shares meant that the twins inherited a large fortune, in spite of the actions of their guardian and trustee Lord Riddell who diverted many of the shares for his own use.

The brothers were educated at Rugby School, referred to as Bugry by Derek and not without reason, for he remained bisexual for much of his life. According to Pam, he said, in horse-racing jargon, 'I ride under both rules'. In the end he settled for women, marrying no less than six of them.

At Rugby the emphasis on Christianity and the Classics, prevalent since the founding of the school by the famous Dr Thomas Arnold, had shifted in favour of the sciences. It was at Rugby that the Jackson twins' love affair with science began and both won important prizes for practical chemistry. It was here also that Derek's interest (an interest which developed into a passion) in spectroscopy began. He became Professor of Spectroscopy at Oxford, was later made a Fellow of the Royal Society and later still an officer of the Legion of Honour. In spite of his other interests, which included fox hunting and horse racing – he rode in the Grand National as an amateur on three occasions – his first love was always science.

The twins were separated only for the second time in their lives (the first was when they were sent to separate prep. schools) when Vivian went to Oriel College, Oxford, and Derek won a scholarship to Trinity College, Cambridge. This was the college where Ernest Rutherford, the first man to split the atom, had been a student, and Derek had access to the Nobel prize-winner at the Cavendish laboratories and at lectures for the Natural Sciences Tripos. After graduation Rutherford asked him to undertake research on a particular aspect of nuclear physics but Derek was determined to work on a subject of his own choosing – investigating properties of the nucleus by means of optical spectroscopy.

Professor Frederick Lindemann of the Clarendon Laboratory in Oxford offered him exactly what he wanted. 'Oxford bought me, just as you might buy a promising yearling,' he confessed, again resorting to racing parlance. Lindemann had taken a risk in appointing a young, unknown scientist to raise the profile of the Clarendon, but he was not disappointed. Aged only 22 Derek produced his seminal paper for the Proceedings of the Royal Society on 'hyperfine structure in the arc spectrum of caesium and nuclear rotation'. It was a scientific breakthrough and earned Derek a place in the history of atomic physics.

Next to his love of science came his love of horses and he was an owner/rider who enjoyed success at race meetings; he came second in the Grand Military Gold Cup at Sandown, a race which still holds considerable prestige, and at his final attempt at the Grand National, when he was 40 and his horse Tulyar was 11, the pair reached the third to last fence where the horse refused to jump after racing in a sea of mud. Hunting was also one of his great delights and while at the Clarendon Laboratory he bought Rignell Hall, near Banbury, where he could keep his hunters and go out with the Heythrop Hunt. It was at Rignell that he and Pam spent the early part of their married life.

Before this, in 1931, Derek had married Poppet John, the teen-age wild child of artist Augustus John, whom he met almost certainly on the hunting field. The marriage did not get off to a good start when after the ceremony, Augustus got into the back of the car with the bride, leaving Derek to sit disconsolately in the front with the chauffeur. Derek and Augustus never got on and this did not help the marriage. 'Neither of these remarkable men saw the point of each other,' wrote Diana Mosley much later. But the marriage was not destined to last. Poppet was young, party-going, promiscuous and somewhat daunted by Derek's way of life. Officially they were mar-ried for five years, but the cracks had appeared long before that.

Derek and Pam married on 29 December 1936 and the very next day tragedy struck. They arrived in Vienna on their honeymoon to find a message for Derek telling him that Vivian had been killed when a sleigh he had been driving overturned in frozen snow at St Moritz. For two days Derek spoke to no one, not even Pam, who later told Diana that part of him had died that day. To lose an identical twin is to lose part of oneself. He never spoke of the accident but the loneliness of the separation remained with him for the rest of his life.

When the Second World War broke out in the autumn of 1939, Derek was at the Clarendon Laboratory which was soon taken over by the Admiralty and he was set to work on the development of radar, then very much in its infancy. Although he always professed his opposition to war with Germany, when war finally broke out he was determined to be part of it and to join the RAF, the only service he considered to be worth fighting in. But his was a reserved occupa-tion and Lindemann refused to let him go. Luckily for Derek, Group Captain Bill Elliot, later to become Air Vice Marshal Elliot, was assistant secretary to the War Cabinet and was also a friend of Pam's. He met Derek and was so impressed by his scientific knowledge, which would be invaluable to the RAF as it entered the radar war, that he persuaded Churchill to prevail on Lindemann to release his protégé. 'He's just the sort of person that England needs and thank God she's got the likes of him – intelligent, determined and full of guts. I'm proud to know him.' With that recommendation Derek joined RAF Loughborough at the time of the fall of France.

He trained first as a gunner but then, after another approach by Pam to Bill Elliot, as a radar operator and navigator in night fighters, training at Middle Wallop in Hampshire. Here he gained a reputation for being imperturbable under pressure and an outstanding interpreter of radar signals and was much in demand by pilots. In June 1941 he was awarded the Distinguished Flying Cross for devotion to duty while successfully operating a secret device (radar) which contributed to the destruction of several enemy aircraft. His accuracy in taking a radar fix was impeccable, as illustrated by the occasion when his suitcase fell out of the aircraft in which he was flying because the hatch was not properly secured. 'Lesser men might have watched its fall; Jackson at once went to his equipment, took a radar fix on his position, and after suitable estimation of the probable trajectory of a suitcase, was able to tell the Wiltshire police exactly where they would find it,' reported the pilot. The suitcase was recovered unopened near Devizes and Derek was greatly relieved because it contained his favourite red silk dressing gown, as well as his change of clothes.

The following year his main work was in 'Window', a system which involved bombers dropping strips of metal foil in order to confuse German radar. He later worked on ways of jamming radio transmissions directing German air defences, much of this done by testing a captured German aircraft. For this work he was promoted to wing commander and there is no doubt that he played a significant part in winning the science war and saving many aircraft from being shot down by enemy fire. In 1944 he was awarded the Air Force Cross and made an OBE at the end of the war. He was also given the Legion of Merit by the government of the USA.

Strange to relate, because of their very different characters and views, Derek formed a lasting friendship with his brother-in-law, Sir Oswald Mosley, who had married Pam's sister Diana in 1936. Derek had little sympathy with some of Mosley's ideas, and he did not attend any of his rallies, but he did agree with Mosley's anti-war position – until he himself became so actively involved in the war against Germany. Even so, he was as anxious as Pam that the two young Mosley sons, Alexander and Max, should be given a home at Rignell while their parents were in prison for their championship of fascism, and was equally insistent that Mosley and Diana should join them there after their release. In the event, they were not allowed to stay there long because of Derek's very secret war work, but they did not leave without a fight on his part. He took it as a personal insult that the Home Secretary, Herbert Morrison, was suggesting he might be a security risk and that his guests might betray secrets to the enemy; he told Morrison so in no uncertain terms, but to no avail. The Mosleys left Rignell to live in a deserted pub at nearby Shipton-under-Wychwood. Derek was the only person who would greet Mosley with an embrace, kissing him on both cheeks – not easy as Mosley was over 6ft tall while Derek was of only medium height – to show his genuine affection.

After the war Derek was outraged at the high level of income tax – 97.5 per cent – which the new Labour government imposed on fortunes as large as his; he was also still resentful about Morrison's attitude to the Mosleys staying at Rignell. When he was offered the post of Professor of Spectroscopy at Oxford in 1948 he decided not to accept. He and Pam immigrated to Ireland and bought Tullamaine Castle, near Fethard in County Tipperary.

The move proved to be a mistake, in spite of the money which Derek saved in taxes. He thoroughly enjoyed the horse-racing side of his life, but he desperately missed his science. He became bored, was unfaithful to Pam on a good many occasions and finally left her for Janetta Kee who had just divorced Robert Kee, the future television presenter. With her he had a daughter called Rose, the only child of all his marriages, with whom he had an uneasy relationship until the final years of his life. This was hardly surprising since he had left Janetta, shortly after Rose was born, to have an affair with Janetta's half-sister, Angela. She had led a colourful life even by the standards of her arty, intellectual, upper-crust circle, and is believed to have been Nancy Mitford's inspiration for Fanny's mother, the Bolter, in *The Pursuit of Love*.

Derek's marriage to Janetta ended in 1956 and his three-year affair with Angela, which had run concurrently for part of that time, ended not long after when he dumped her for another woman. Janetta and Angela, unsurprisingly, did not speak for twenty-seven years. They were reunited in 1980 at Tramores, the house in southern Spain which Derek had paid for Angela to build.

Derek's fourth wife was Consuelo Regina Maria Eyre, who called herself Princess Ratibor, having previously been married to a central European prince. She apparently felt she could tame this eccentric and volatile man and convert him to the Roman Catholic faith. When Pam heard, through Diana, that he was taking instruction from a priest, she said: 'I feel so sorry for the priest.' Derek and Consuelo were married in 1957 but the marriage lasted less than two years, after which Derek paid her off with 'a lot of diamonds'.

Derek's fifth marriage to Barbara Skelton was even more bizarre. She had been married to journalist Cyril Connolly and then to publisher George Weidenfeld. Connolly divorced her for adultery, citing Weidenfeld; then Weidenfeld divorced her, citing Connolly, with whom she then resumed a relationship. Not surprisingly, this gave her the nickname Helter Skelter. She also had affairs with other men, including King Farouk of Egypt and journalist Kenneth Tynan. She was a volatile, rude and aggressive woman and her marriage to Derek in 1966 soon degenerated into angry and violent behaviour. As ever, he gave her a generous divorce settlement but there must have been times when he regretted parting from gentle Pam, with whom he was now on very good terms again.

He was soon to sail into calmer waters when in 1967, shortly after his divorce from Barbara, he married Marie-Christine Reille, a good-looking French widow in her thirties. This marriage lasted for fourteen years – the same as his marriage to Pam – and ended only with his death. Derek and Marie-Christine had a shared interest in racehorse breeding and also in art. They went to live in Switzerland but Derek continued his research in spectroscopy in Paris, publishing several important papers. They also kept long-haired dachshunds as Pam and Derek had done. Could this have been another reason why the marriage lasted so long? In addition, Derek at last got to know his daughter Rose and her baby son Rollo; Rose took a flat nearby in Lausanne so that she could visit him in the final months of his life. He died of a heart attack caused by clotting of the arteries, having had a leg amputated, in 1982.

Derek Jackson was a man of extreme contradictions. Meticulous in his work, the same was not true of his personal relationships. Though vehemently opposed to the war with Germany, he became one of his country's war heroes. He had immense charm which could turn to anger in a split second and when angry he could be extremely rude. He never wanted children and only had one child from all his six marriages, yet he was devoted to his nephews, nieces and stepchildren, as well as, very late in life, to Rose and his only grandson Rollo. At the time of the break-up of their marriage he was very unkind to Pam, but they soon became friends and remained so until his death. He also remained close to Pam's family, especially the Mosleys, and after he died Diana spoke of him as being 'such good company, a truly brilliant and wonderful man – though not entirely human'.

An appreciation of Derek Jackson is incomplete without a transcript of a conversation between him and a young English delegate to a conference on nuclear physics, which took place near Rome in the 1970s. He and Derek were discussing their colleagues at the congress during an afternoon break:

Delegate: I'm told there is one extraordinary fellow here. English, too, though he lived abroad for years.
Derek: Really. Who's that?
Delegate: Well, he's not only a brilliant physicist – he also had an outstanding war in the RAF, winning lots of decorations, and before and

after the war he rode three times in the Grand National. He's got pots of money – through a family shareholding in the *News of the World*, of all things – and has been married at least half a dozen times, including to one of those Mitford girls.

Derek: I think I ought to tell you, before you go any further, that I'm the man in question.

Delegate: Oh, really? I'm sorry, but we haven't been introduced.

Derek: I'm Derek Jackson.

Delegate (after a pause): No, that wasn't the name.

The shrieks of laughter which this story must have caused when related to the Mitford sisters by Derek can only be imagined.

Seven

The Turbulent Thirties

At the beginning of the 1930s, although the turmoil in the financial markets was continuing to grow, David and Sydney could be reasonably content with the activities of their large and lively family. But the storm clouds were gathering for them, as they were for the world at large.

For Nancy, at least, life had temporarily taken a more settled turn – though it was not to last. Hamish finally broke off their 'engagement' by telling her that he was engaged to someone else (this was not true but Nancy, who never admitted that he was homosexual, believed him). She was devastated, but only weeks later she accepted a proposal of marriage from Peter Rodd, who had been a friend of Hamish's at Oxford. It was not a wise choice. Peter was not in love with Nancy any more than she was with him. He had been sent down from Oxford and had failed in every job he had attempted. He was extravagant, a heavy drinker and, worst of all, pedantic and boring – about the worst sin in the Mitford family. Nevertheless, he was blonde, good-looking and his socialist politics fitted in with what Nancy believed at the time. The wedding took place in London in 1933 and the couple went to live in Chiswick where Nancy enjoyed, for a time, being a married woman. *Highland Fling*, her first novel, had been published in 1931 and went into a second edition; she had followed it with *Christmas Pudding* the following year.

Meanwhile, Pam was making a good fist of running the farm at Biddesden in very difficult times, but all was not well with Bryan and Diana. Diana had begun to feel that her wealthy and glamorous life-style and even her two little boys, Jonathan and Desmond, were not enough to occupy her lively mind. She felt that there must be more to life but was unsure what that might be. Then in 1932 she met Sir Oswald Mosley at a party and fell in love with him. From then on her life took an entirely different turn.

Mosley was an enigmatic figure who had been both a Conservative and Labour MP but, dissatisfied with both main political parties, had then formed his own, the New Party, which failed to get support in the general election of 1931. When he and Diana met he was about to launch the British Union of Fascists (BUF). Diana fell in love both with the man and his ideas and was prepared to sacrifice her life-style and her reputation for him; this was in spite of the fact that he was already married to Cynthia, known as Cimmie, daughter of Lord Curzon, and was known to be a serial womaniser.

The Redesdales were horrified but Diana was not to be dissuaded. She and Bryan were divorced the following year and she lived in a house in Eaton Square, London, known as the Eatonry by the family. Her younger sisters were forbidden to go there, her beloved Tom refused to visit, Pam stayed on to help on the Biddesden farm and only Nancy was a regular visitor. Diana did not expect Mosley to divorce Cimmie, with whom he had three children, but she needed to be available whenever he could visit her. Just before Diana's divorce came through, Cimmie died of peritonitis – some said that because of her husband's womanising she had lost the will to live, though if penicillin had been available she would have been saved. Diana and Mosley were shocked and the grief-stricken Mosley threw himself into building up the increasingly violent and disreputable BUF and – almost unbelievably – embarked on an affair with Cimmie's younger sister, Alexandra 'Baba' Metcalfe, whom he took on holiday to France.

Unsurprisingly, Diana was not happy with this arrangement but the die was already cast; in any case, she had come so far that there was no going back. Having received an invitation to visit Germany from Putzi Hanfstaengl, Hitler's foreign press secretary whom she had met at a party in London, she left England for Germany in August 1933, taking Unity with her. Unity, having joined the BUF when she had met Mosley through Diana, had now espoused a cause which would take over and ultimately take her life. Filled with fascist zeal, the sisters embarked on their first visit to Hitler's Germany. David and Sydney were unaware that Unity had also become a member of the party so the visit to Germany seemed a good opportunity for their wayward daughter to learn the language.

Although Putzi was unable to organise a meeting with Hitler for the girls, he did get them tickets to the Parteitag in Nuremberg, a four-day celebration of the Nazis coming to power. They saw Hitler from a distance and were struck by the intense feeling of excitement in the crowd when he appeared. They were both immensely impressed by the massive parades which showed how Nazism had restored the faith of a country which had been utterly crushed in 1918. Diana particularly must have compared Germany with England and its ineffective governments, and these orderly marches with the BUF rally which Mosley had organised at Olympia. These had ended in violence when infiltrated by communists, losing Mosley most of the favourable press coverage he had hitherto received.

For Unity it was like lighting a blue touchpaper. To meet Hitler, whom she now regarded as 'the greatest man of all time', and to embrace Nazism became the sole aims in her life. Always obsessive, she now had a cause for that obsession. She persuaded her parents to let her go back to Germany with the excuse of learning the language properly, omitting to tell them that the real reason for this was so she could communicate with Hitler. She lived mostly in Munich until the outbreak of war, lodging first with an elderly woman who ran a finishing school for young ladies wanting to learn German and later in a succession of flats, the final one being obtained for her by Hitler, the young Jewish couple who had lived there having 'gone abroad'. Like so many fanatics, Unity refused to see the horrors of Hitler's regime.

Unity had engineered her first meeting with Hitler by sitting hour on hour in the Osteria Bavaria, a restaurant which he and his henchmen frequented. Eventually her patience was rewarded. Hitler had noticed the tall, blonde, blue-eyed English girl, the model of the Aryan woman, and invited her to his table. Trembling with excitement, she had the first of over 100 meetings with the Führer, with whom she became close friends. She was undoubtedly in love with him but he was not much interested in women as sexual objects and it is virtually certain that they never became lovers. It is more likely that he particularly enjoyed the friendship of this exuberant, amusing and attractive English girl who was not afraid to contradict and tease him, unlike the yes-men with whom he had surrounded himself.

The British press had a field day when the news of Unity's friendship with Hitler became common knowledge, especially after she wrote a letter to the German newspaper *Der Stürmer* in which she confessed to being a Jew-hater. It was certainly no secret since she was proud of her German connection but it must have been torture for David and Sydney, even though they and also Tom had met Hitler and been impressed by what he had done for Germany.

Diana and Tom were photographed at Hitler's rallies, but what was kept a secret was Diana's marriage to Mosley. This took place in 1936 in the Berlin house of Joseph Goebbels and his wife Magda, with whom both girls had become friends, and with Hitler as a guest. The secrecy was for several reasons: to protect Mosley's image, to keep the news from Baba Metcalfe with whom he was still having an affair, but mainly to keep from the press Diana's visits to Germany for the purpose of setting up a commercial radio station; the aim of this was to broadcast from Germany to southern England (in those days there were no such British stations) in order to raise money for the BUF whose funds were running low. After much negotiation Diana did finally get Hitler's permission to set up such a station, but the outbreak of war meant that it never happened. The marriage was finally disclosed when the Mosleys' eldest son Alexander was born in 1938.

Nancy had not been idle while her sisters embraced fascism. She and Peter, who became known in the family as 'Prod', had attended several BUF rallies and bought black shirts – the symbol of Mosley's followers – but Nancy was too much of a tease to become a fanatic. Such people, she felt, had to be made fun of. She did this in her third book, *Wigs on the Green*, which was published in 1935 and in which the heroine, Eugenia Malmains, is very obviously modelled on Unity. This caused Diana and Nancy to be 'non-speakers' for four years and Unity swore she would never speak to Nancy again but failed to carry out her threat. Diana and Unity could both be teasing and mocking in other respects, but woe betide anyone who made fun of Mosley or Hitler.

The activities of their elder daughters may have caused the Redesdales to take their eyes off the ball as far as Jessica was concerned. Aged 16, Jessica and her first cousin Ann Farrer, known as Idden in Boudledidge, travelled to Paris to study at the Sorbonne and also, unknown to their parents, to enjoy the delights of the city, including visiting the Folies Bergère. When she returned to England she, like all the others, went through her debutante season and confessed, much against her will, to be rather enjoying herself. But like Diana and Unity, Jessica was forming opinions which would soon lead to an obsession as great as theirs and further tear the family apart.

In the early 1930s Jessica had become interested in politics, although her views were in a totally opposite direction to those Diana and Unity eventually espoused. When she read Beverley Nichols' book *Cry Havoc*, which described the worst horrors of the First World War and the growing social and financial problems in Europe, together with the communist manifesto, the unformed ideas which had been in her mind suddenly clicked into place and she began to champion the extreme left-wing politics which obsessed her for the rest of her life.

Jessica's socialist ideas were further hardened when she read *The Brown Book of Hitler Terror*, which described the rounding-up of communists and other opponents of Nazism after the burning of the Reichstag building; a time when many were beaten and some murdered. But it was when she read a book called *Out of Bounds: the Education of Giles and Esmond Romilly* that she began to find a serious reason for putting her ideas into practice. The Romilly brothers were cousins both of the Mitfords and the Churchills, and for several years Jessica had worshipped Esmond and his left-wing activities. He had started a magazine attacking public schools and had run away from Wellington College aged 16 and gone to work in a left-wing London bookshop but she had never had the chance to meet him. When they finally met by chance early in 1937, at the weekend house party of another cousin, she couldn't believe her luck.

Esmond had been fighting in the Spanish Civil War on the side of the left-wing International Brigade and was planning to return as a war correspondent for the *News Chronicle*. He didn't need much persuading to take his pretty and committed cousin with him. Jessica forged a letter from some friends asking her to go on holiday with them in Europe, so that her parents would not suspect for some time where she had actually gone, and the cousins simply disappeared to Spain. When the Redesdales found out they were distraught and so were the rest of the family, who all gathered at the London house in Rutland Gate to decide how to get Jessica back. Unity 'scrammed back' from Germany, Pam and Derek came from Oxfordshire and Prod told everyone what he thought they ought to do. Even Churchill and the Foreign Office were involved: Foreign Secretary Anthony Eden informed the British consul in Bilbao and allowed Nancy and Peter to travel in a naval destroyer to persuade the runaways to come home. This they refused to do and finally the Redesdales agreed to them being married (they were both underage and needed parental permission) in Bayonne on 18 May 1937; the long-suffering Sydney, as usual making the best of a bad job, was in attendance. The newspapers had yet another field day – 'Peer's Daughter Elopes to Spain' and 'Mixed Up Mitford Girls Still Confusing Europe' were only two. The *Daily Express* lived to regret its scoop since it confused Jessica with Debo: Debo sued for libel and settled out of court for £1,000 which she spent on a fur coat.

Jessica had told her mother that she was pregnant before the marriage took place which was another good reason for her parents to allow it. The couple returned from Spain to London later in the summer, rented a house in Rotherhithe in London's East End and the baby, Julia, was born just before Christmas. The new parents, despite their irresponsible behaviour on many fronts, were besotted with their daughter; they were heartbroken when she died of pneumonia, following a measles attack, aged only 5 months old. In February 1939, faced with mounting bills at home, they left for the United States on the understanding that in the event of war with Germany, Esmond would return home to fight.

Jessica's running away and consequential marriage had a more divisive effect on the family than either Diana's or Unity's activities. Diana and Jessica never made contact again until Nancy was dying in the 1970s. With the exception of Tom, Esmond refused to see Jessica's family, whom he regarded as fascists, and she had to meet them secretly. Perhaps surprisingly, Jessica and Unity never gave up on each other – they were too good friends for that – and it is possible that, although they were so diametrically opposed politically, each recognised and accepted the commitment of the other. For David and Sydney, Jessica's behaviour took its toll and made them feel even more beleaguered by their headline-provoking family.

For Debo, who together with Pam and Tom never gave her parents any cause for anxiety, the latter half of the 1930s was as traumatic as for any of the family. Swinbrook House, hated by the others but loved by her since she had spent most of her childhood there, was sold in 1936 because the state of David's finances in the Depression made its upkeep impossible. They moved to Old Mill Cottage on the outskirts of High Wycombe, causing the family to chant, 'from Batsford Mansion to Asthall Manor, to Swinbrook House, to Old Mill Cottage' as an indication of their declining fortunes. Only Debo and Jessica moved there with their parents; at the end of 1936 Pam married Derek Jackson with whom Debo, aged 15, imagined herself in love. But Jessica's flight to Spain, which she kept a secret even from her youngest sister, was a body blow for Debo. This was something which Jessica never realised and it also meant that Debo was often alone with nanny and the governess at Old Mill Cottage, which she hated. The cruise on which Sydney had planned to take the three younger girls early in 1937, and to which Debo was looking forward, was inevitably cancelled; she was not allowed to go to Jessica's wedding either and thereafter was only able to meet her occasionally because she and Esmond did not see eye to eye.

Added to this, as the decade progressed, the deterioration of relations between her parents became more obvious. Although both of them had at first been impressed by Hitler and what he was doing for Germany, David eventually did a U-turn and the Germans once more became 'beastly Huns' to him; Sydney meanwhile stuck to her guns. Like Pam, Debo was apolitical, but the atmosphere which her parents' opposing views inevitably created rubbed off on her, the only child left at home. She deserved that fur coat.

It was not all misery for Debo, however, because in 1938, just after her debutante season had ended, she met and fell in love with Lord Andrew Cavendish, the younger son of the Duke of Devonshire, to whom she later became engaged.

The tragedies of the turbulent thirties were not yet over for the Redesdales. Unity had vowed to shoot herself if her two beloved countries, England and Germany, went to war with one another, though she felt that Hitler's admiration for England meant he would never attack. There was great relief when Prime Minister Neville Chamberlain came back from meeting Hitler in Munich in 1938, claiming that he had achieved Peace with Honour.

But Hitler had no intention of keeping his side of the agreement. In March 1939 he invaded Czechoslovakia and then, ignoring warnings from Britain, followed this with an invasion of Poland at the beginning of September. Britain and France declared war on Germany on 3 September. That same day, Unity went to the English Garden in Munich, took out her ivory-handled pistol and shot herself in the head.

Eight

Woman the Wife

Diana Mosley once remarked that Derek Jackson had been in love with most of the Mitfords, including Tom. He and Pam had first met at Biddesden while she was running the Guinnesses' farm and it is possible that he chose her because she was the most readily available. In fact, it turned out to be one of the better choices he made in his private life. Her kind and calm nature combined with her housewifely skills made her the ideal wife for Derek at this most frenetic time of his career: he was at the cutting edge of the scientific world, had a particularly exacting role with the RAF during the war, to say nothing of his horse-racing exploits. Unlike Derek, Pam was neither clever, creative nor complex, but her lifelong friend, writer James Lees-Milne, paid tribute to her 'nobility of character and unadulterated goodness', adding that she was also quite unaware of her own beauty. No one who knew her would argue with him.

Pam moved into Rignell Hall with Derek in the autumn of 1936, anticipating his forthcoming divorce from Poppet John by a few months, and it was from here that they drove to High Wycombe, where the Redesdale family was now living, to announce their engagement.

Fifteen-year-old Deborah, who had met Derek on the hunting field and imagined herself in love with him, fainted on hearing the news.

Derek was madly in love with Pam, as his letters during their courtship show beyond doubt. This one was written early in 1936 while she was motoring in Austria:

> Darling, you are so wonderful and beautiful and I adore you and always will; all the time I am not with you is not only time wasted, it is time spent in misery … You are the whole world for me and nothing else matters at all. How I wish I could see your darling blue eyes now … Darling, you are everything in the world to me, and every moment away from you is dead to me.

Pam and Derek were married in London, at Carlton registry office, on 29 December 1936, while the British were still reeling over the abdication of Edward VIII. Pam was 'laden with jewels which her generous husband had showered upon her' but in their wedding photograph all the women appear to be wearing black. This, however, was a trend for smart occasions in those days because London in winter was often beset by filthy smog – a mixture of smoke (before the introduction of smokeless fuel) and fog – which made light colours look grubby within minutes. No one is smiling, though this may be because it was not the fashion at that time to smile for formal photographs. With hindsight, this somewhat funereal picture might be said to be prophetic, for within hours of it being taken Derek's twin brother Vivian, who mysteriously was not at the wedding, was killed in a sleigh accident in Switzerland, an event which scarred Derek's life forever.

Pam and Derek settled down (if this mercurial man could ever be said to settle anywhere) at Rignell, a former hunting lodge with distant views over the Heythrop country. Diana had once described the house as hideous and the interior decor became something of a laughing stock among the Mitford family. Derek's taste was for Heal's furniture and bright contrasting colours. The main bedroom had pink walls and green furniture which he said were the colours of apple trees in spring. He had taken great trouble to reproduce the exact colours and Pam must have liked them because she kept one of the green chests of drawers in her bedroom all her life. When Pam and Derek moved to Tullamaine Castle in County Tipperary after the war, Pam set about redecorating the rooms. Lady Redesdale was the first of the family to visit her there and was later asked what it was like by one of the other sisters. 'I'm not going to say,' was her tactful reply.

One of the things which bound this very different couple together was their love of horses and dogs. Their particular passion was for long-haired dachshunds which were probably a substitute for the children Pam never had. Derek did not want children and made his views on the matter clear, but even so, Pam underwent gynaecological surgery in 1937. Clearly this was not successful because although she became pregnant at least twice, she never carried a child to full term. Meanwhile, they acquired Wuda, their first long-haired dachshund who later presented them with puppies, which were called Hamelin and Weser from the story of the Pied Piper. They were the first of a succession of dachshunds, the last of which died many years later just before Pam returned from Switzerland to live in England. Early in the marriage a trip to Paris was cancelled when Pam and Derek, on their way to the boat train, realised that they had left their tickets behind. When they drove back to Rignell to get them, Wuda jumped into the back seat as soon as the butler opened the door and gave them such a pleading look that they changed their plans and spent the weekend with Wuda instead of at Claridges (Derek's favourite hotel).

Shortly before the outbreak of war Derek and Pam went to America on a visit arranged through Derek's boss, Professor Lindemann, on behalf of the Admiralty. This trip gave them the opportunity to visit Jessica and her husband Esmond, who had by now settled in the US. Pam often made surprise visits to her sisters as their letters to one another show and this was no exception. 'I was amazed at Woman turning up here,' Jessica wrote to her mother. The sisters were delighted to see one another but Derek and Esmond did not get on; also, Pam was very worried when Jessica told her that they hid their money between the pages of books. She was sure that they would forget where it was or leave it behind when they left.

Esmond, however, was fascinated when he learned that they planned to fly back to England. Since June 1939 the Americans had operated a transatlantic flying boat service which carried up to seventeen civilian passengers. On 4 August a British service began to operate and Derek booked them in on the second trip in a Caribou flying boat. Pam wrote to Jessica:

> Our flying journey was wonderful, but rather frightening when we took off. The plane seemed far too small to battle across the Atlantic. We came down at Botwood in Newfoundland, and were able to go for a walk while the plane was being filled up with petrol. The next stop was at Foynes in Ireland. The whole journey only took 28 hours!

Her matter-of-fact description is another example of the quiet, largely unknown Mitford sister's courage and spirit of adventure. She would probably have been one of the first 100 women to fly the Atlantic, but she took it entirely in her stride.

Unsurprisingly, the journey caused something of a stir and before they boarded the seaplane, journalists were waiting to question them about the purpose of their journey. 'We are in rather a hurry to get home for our little dog's birthday tomorrow,' said Derek, in what must have been a particularly convincing fashion. However much they loved the dogs – during their stay in America they had a competition each morning to see who would wake first and sing good morning to the dachshunds back home – the truth was that Derek was carrying top-secret papers, which he refused to trust to the diplomatic bag in case they should fall into the hands of the Russians.

Horses, too, played a big part in their lives, both in the hunting and racing worlds. Pam had got to know Derek well while he was riding to hounds with the Heythrop Hunt with which he went out frequently; another of his passions was to ride as an amateur in National Hunt races where he enjoyed fair success. He kept most of his horses with trainer Bay Powell and Pam would often accompany him to Powell's yard near Aldbourne when he went to ride them out on the downs. She also looked after those which were kept at Rignell and it is very obvious from his letters before and during the war that Derek entrusted them to her care. In August 1940 he wrote to say: 'I am writing to Bay [Powell] to have all the horses sent home. They will have to stay out all winter – buy oats and hay.' In February 1941 he was advising her to 'have the two-year-olds back as soon as the weather seems to get warmer', and when she told Derek about a colt with an injured leg, he said that it should only be led out enough to get the swelling down, and not turned out.

In their love letters Derek would often assume the character of a horse and at the end of one letter, written in January 1936, he drew a miserable-looking horse above the words, 'the poor Derek horse is crying because you aren't here to stroke it'. He would always sign himself Derek (H-D) for Horse of Dog, the pet name they used together, sending, of course, his love to the DDs (darling dogs) and later the dds (their puppies). In the years after their divorce, when they had become friends again, their letters continued to convey their shared love of horses and dogs (especially dachshunds), and at their last meeting, at the wedding of Debo's daughter Sophy at Chatsworth in 1979, it seemed entirely natural that Pam should greet Derek with the words, 'Hello Horse'.

As well as their love of horses and dogs, Pam proved to be a good wife to Derek because she had all the homely qualities that most of her sisters lacked. Nancy, perhaps now rather envious of the sister she had once treated so cruelly, wrote to family friend Mrs Hammersley (known as Mrs Ham): 'Pam lives in a round of boring gaiety of the neighbourly description but even so I envy a country existence of almost any kind and feel certain I shall never achieve one.' But Pam had her own worries, about food and petrol rationing and about blacking out the windows at Rignell. 'We have had to make black curtains for *all* the windows. Even if a pinprick of light shows the police come rushing down on you!' she wrote to Jessica at the end of September 1939. It was so typical of Pam to worry about domestic matters like blackout curtains while still being terribly anxious about Unity, who had disappeared after trying to take her life in Munich. Her whereabouts were not discovered until the beginning of October.

Always able to look on the bright side, Pam describes a visit to London, where 'we saw barrage balloons for the first time. They are so very beautiful and make a wonderful decoration.' Her greatest sadness was having to give up her herd of Aberdeen Angus cattle due to the lack of cattle feed. 'It is very sad because I bred some really beautiful ones. However they will make good beef. The bull, Black Hussar, has already been sent to the butcher. Poor Black Hussar!' she wrote to Jessica in June 1941.

She was also anxious about Derek's determination to join the RAF, even though it was she who had made this possible; but once he was accepted she took on the role of a service wife with her usual equanimity, sending such essentials as boot polish, button polish, a pillow and warm clothes. At this time she managed to cook tasty meals from next to nothing and there was always a plenteous supply of eggs both at Rignell and also in Stanmore; Derek was stationed at Stanmore for a short time in 1942 where she joined him and brought with her some chickens. By strange coincidence, her sister Deborah and Andrew Cavendish, later to be the Duke of Devonshire, were also living in Stanmore (also with chickens), as was Pam's lifelong friend Margaret Budd, whose husband George was in the same squadron as Derek.

Derek wrote to Pam at the end of the war to say how much he was looking forward to sampling smoke-cured bacon from a pig killed at Rignell, and which he could be sure Pam would cook to perfection. As hostilities were finally drawing to a close, Pam looked after a cow called Holly which Derek's boss at the Clarendon Laboratory, Professor Lindemann (now Lord Cherwell), had acquired in order to have a constant supply of milk and cream. He had a bizarre diet of olive oil, dairy products and eggs (which came from the Rignell farm) and Derek would take the latter two into Oxford twice a week for him. Pam was very happy to keep the skim milk for the calves.

Her qualities of good housekeeping and parsimony in wartime are perhaps best summed up by her joyous remark to Diana when peace was finally declared: 'Well, Nard, VE Day and the Bromo has lasted!' Bromo was the finest lavatory paper, described by its manufacturers as being 'unsurpassed in quality and purity because it has been cooked for hours until it is of the consistency necessary for toilet paper'. And Pam still had some left with which to start the austerity period …

Nine

The War and its Consequences

For nearly a month the family in England had no news of Unity since communications between England and Germany were severed. Then in early October they received a letter from Teddy von Almasy, brother of Janos, who lived in neutral Budapest. He told them that Unity was ill in hospital but was recovering; he later cabled them to say that she was making good progress, but more than this they could not discover. Then in November they heard from the American Embassy that Unity was in hospital where she was recovering from a suicide attempt. The papers went wild with stories which were generally far from the mark, and finally, on Christmas Eve, David and Sydney had a telephone call from Janos; he was in Switzerland with Unity, who had been sent there by Hitler in a special ambulance carriage attached to a train. He handed the phone to Unity. 'When are you coming to get me?' she pleaded.

In spite of it being Christmas, David managed to get hold of the necessary travel documents and Sydney and Debo set off for Switzerland three days later. It was a freezing cold, miserable journey with no trains running on time. Sydney and Debo were appalled by Unity's appearance. She was very thin and pale and her hair was matted around her head wound. Worse still, she had a vacant expression and she remembered some things but not others. 'She was like someone who had had a stroke,' Debo recalled. But she recognised them and was delighted to see them. It turned out that Hitler had paid for her hospital treatment.

Then began the traumatic task of getting Unity home. The journey was cold and took forever and Unity was so very ill. To make matters worse the press were waiting for them at Calais. 'The Girl Who Loved Hitler' was not going to escape them until they had heard her dramatic story. Sydney was offered £5,000 for the story which, of course, she declined. By now they had missed the boat and had to stay overnight in a Calais hotel and sail the following morning. David was waiting anxiously at Folkestone with an ambulance and as Unity appeared on a stretcher, he rushed up to embrace her, all differences forgotten.

They were not yet free of the press who besieged them again as they tried to leave the port. Then the ambulance broke down and they had to spend the night in a hotel, suspecting that the vehicle had been tampered with deliberately. Finally, they arrived home – in this case, High Wycombe – where Unity rested before being admitted to hospital in Oxford.

The doctors told Sydney that everything had been done for Unity in Germany and only time could improve her condition now. In fact, although she improved greatly, she never progressed further than the age of 12, she was prone to violent rages, was very clumsy and was incontinent at night. Sydney now made it her life's work to look after her and a hard task it proved to be. Eventually she, Debo and Unity moved to Old Mill Cottage in Swinbrook where Unity knew her way around and was known and accepted by the local people. She would have liked to take her to the remote Scottish island of Inch Kenneth, which David had bought with some of the proceeds from the sale of Swinbrook, but the authorities would not allow people with the views of Sydney and Unity to live on an offshore island in wartime. Unity achieved a degree of independence and could travel to London alone, do her collage and re-taught herself to write, but the funny, eccentric, attractive Unity had gone forever.

The outbreak of war meant much unusual activity for Nancy. Prod joined the army which meant that they didn't have to see too much of one another and she was left to her own devices; playing at being a married woman had lost much of its charm. At this time she wrote another book, *Pigeon Pie*, which was not a huge success but made her some much-needed money. She also began working for the Air Raid Precautions unit (ARP) in Praed Street, Paddington, and was later asked to broadcast a series of lectures on fire fighting. These were later discontinued because many of those who listened found the famous 'Mitford voice' so irritating that they wanted to put Nancy on the fire. Even so, a very different Nancy was emerging from the one who had told Pam in 1926, when they had run the canteen for strike-breakers, that she couldn't manage anything to do with ovens – 'one's poor hands'.

So seriously did she take her role as a citizen in wartime England that she informed on Diana, telling Gladwyn Jebb at the Ministry of Economic Affairs that her sister was an extremely dangerous person who had made many visits to Germany shortly before the war (she did not know about the radio station negotiations). Mosley was already in Brixton prison for his British Union of Fascists activities and soon Diana was arrested and taken to Holloway, where she remained until 1943. Nancy later told the authorities that Pam and Derek were dangerous fascists, but this was never taken further as it was obvious that it was very wide of the mark, and probably the result of one of Derek's teases.

Nancy did, however, stoically stay in London throughout the bombing and grew vegetables in her garden to supplement her rations. Later she ran a hostel for homeless Jewish women at the family home in Rutland Gate, much to the disgust of Sydney who was still pro-Hitler and anti-Semitic.

Nancy's contact with the intelligence services led to her being asked to do some information-gathering at the Free French Officers' Club, where she met and had an affair with an officer called Andre Roy. This resulted in an ectopic pregnancy, after which she was unable to bear children. Meanwhile, she got a job at Heywood Hill's bookshop in Curzon Street which became a meeting place for her friends, who included Lord Berners, Lady Cunard, the Sitwells, Cecil Beaton, Evelyn Waugh and any of the Mitford family who happened to be in London at the time. She loved her time there even though it coincided with the V-1 bombings; it was also around this time that she met the man who was to become the great love of her life.

Colonel Gaston Palewski was General Charles de Gaulle's right-hand man. He was wealthy, sophisticated and sexually, rather than physically, attractive. Nancy fell for him hook, line and sinker as Diana had for Mosley, Unity for Hitler, Jessica for Esmond and, in her much more understated way, Pam for Derek. Her lifelong passion for him was not returned, although after their initial relationship they remained close friends for the rest of Nancy's life. Due to her deep feelings for him she was able to write, without the brittleness of her previous work, a novel which became an instant bestseller and secured her position as a literary figure and made her financially independent.

The Pursuit of Love is semi-autobiographical. The Radlett family is loosely based on the Mitfords, with Uncle Matthew and Aunt Sadie having many of the same characteristics as David and Sydney. Linda is close to Nancy and Fabrice to the Colonel; like Jessica, Jassy hoards her running away money, and kind, sensible Fanny, the 'I' of the story, though supposed to be based on a cousin, Billa Harrod, has in my opinion many of the characteristics of Pam. *The Pursuit of Love* is a witty, tightly written novel which is very different from Nancy's earlier offerings. The book and its sequel, *Love in a Cold Climate*, lightweight and frothy though they may seem, are literary masterpieces. Nancy richly deserved her success.

The Pursuit of Love was published in 1945 and in the autumn Nancy went to Paris with the purpose of doing business on behalf of the bookshop. Literary success and true love had brought her the sort of happiness she had never felt before. She was jubilant at Atlee's election victory, as she had always been socialist at heart, but she soon decided to make her home in France. In many ways Nancy's war was the making of her.

The same could hardly be said for Diana, though she endured the privations of Holloway with remarkable stoicism and made a life for herself and Mosley when the war was over. When she was imprisoned, Max, her youngest son, was 11 weeks old and had yet to be weaned. She chose not to take him to prison with her, fearing that he would succumb to infection in the filth of Holloway, but this meant, although she did not know it at the time since she expected to be released within days, that she only saw her children intermittently for the next three and a half years. The food in prison was grim, she was allowed only limited visits from her family, and letters were similarly restricted and strictly censored.

Family letters and visits kept her going. Sydney, despite the time spent caring for Unity, managed to visit once a week, braving the bombs and enduring inefficient transport in order to see her daughter, bringing eggs and vegetables to supplement her woefully inadequate diet. Pam also visited, as well as giving a home to Alexander, Max and the formidable Nanny Higgs, and later Diana was able to have visits from her children, her other sisters and from Mosley himself. She and Mosley appeared separately before an Advisory Committee at which they were examined by Norman, later Lord, Birkett who was to be one of the judges at the Nuremberg Trials. Since neither were prepared to renounce their views, it was deemed necessary to keep them in prison.

Diana got on well with the other prisoners, since she never tried to play the fine lady, and also with her warders. 'We've never had such laughs since Lady Mosley left,' declared her favourite warder, Miss Davies, much later.

Eventually, Mosley was permitted to join Diana in Holloway, mainly thanks to Tom who asked Churchill if this would be possible. Home Secretary Herbert Morrison opposed it, but Churchill pressed his point and the Mosleys were able to occupy part of the Preventative Detention Block in Holloway. All their children were allowed to visit, Diana was given their rations to cook with, instead of prison food, and Mosley grew vegetables in the prison garden. They stayed in this 'suite', as it was described by a hostile press, for two years and then Mosley contracted serious phlebitis from a First World War wound.

It became so bad that it was feared he could die and, rather than have a martyr like Mosley on their hands, the government released the couple at the end of 1943.

They were received with open arms by Pam and Derek at Rignell and Pam became 'Wonderwoman' by dealing with the press corps which camped outside the house as soon as the Mosleys' whereabouts were discovered. Nevertheless, Derek's work was top secret so Herbert Morrison would not allow them to stay in spite of Derek's protests. They moved to a partly disused pub not far away where Diana had to clean and cook, making the meagre rations go round the family.

Later they moved to Crux Easton in Hampshire and then to Crowood, near Ramsbury, in Wiltshire. Diana made both houses attractive, even in wartime, as only she knew how, and they were visited by all the family and friends like Lord Berners, who never wavered in his loyalty to Diana.

When Jessica and Esmond arrived in New York they first enjoyed the luxury of the Shelton Hotel while they contacted several influential people whose names they had been given, the most useful being Katherine Graham whose father, Eugene Meyer, owned the *Washington Post*. Jessica and Katherine became good friends and Meyer later lent Esmond $1,000 to buy a liquor licence for the very successful cocktail bar he was running in Miami. Before this, however, Jessica and Esmond took a variety of jobs while being welcomed into New York society, where their entertaining personalities made them poplar wherever they went. Jessica still missed Unity, her favourite sister, and, in spite of their political differences, she refused to speak to the American press when the news of Unity's attempted suicide became known. Her greatest sadness was that she could never talk about her feelings for Unity with Esmond, who thought of her – and the rest of the family – as rabid fascists.

While he was successfully selling silk stockings in Washington and serving cocktails in Miami, Esmond was watching the situation in Europe carefully because the congenial life he and Jessica were living in America had in no way diminished his determination to fight for his country when it became necessary. By the summer of 1940 he knew that the time was ripe and he travelled to Halifax, Nova Scotia, to join the Canadian Royal Air Force. Jessica enrolled for a stenography course, which was to stand her in good stead for the rest of her life, and stayed with friends in Washington. What Esmond didn't know was that Jessica was pregnant again.

Having gained a commission as a pilot officer, Esmond was sent to Europe. In February Jessica gave birth to a baby daughter who was christened Constancia but always nicknamed Dinkydonk, Dinky or just The Donk after the donkey which was the symbol of the Democratic Party. As she grew up, Dinky developed the womanly qualities which reminded Jessica of Pam.

In early December 1941 Jessica and Dinky were due to travel to England to be with Esmond, but just before they left Jessica received a telegram to say that he was missing on active service. For a long time she refused to believe he had been killed, but eventually she accepted that he had drowned in the North Sea. She decided not to return to England and vented her anger on the Mosleys (but never on Unity), whose views she felt were responsible for the situation in Europe.

Six months after Esmond's death, Jessica got a job with the Office of Price Administration (OAP) which was responsible for wartime rationing policy. She was rapidly promoted and found herself working for a Jewish lawyer named Bob Treuhaft, whom she later married. They had both moved to California and they were married there in secret because Jessica didn't want the press getting hold of yet another Mitford story, particularly in view of the anti-Semitic members of her family. But a letter which she wrote to Churchill after the Mosleys' release from jail, demanding that they should be re-imprisoned, alerted the press to her whereabouts and she and Bob spent several days hiding in their apartment with the blinds drawn. She later regretted the tone of her letter but in the short term it led to her being asked to join the Communist Party. She and Bob both rose in the party ranks and for the next few years Decca's life was devoted to the party and the Civil Rights Movement. In 1944 she gave birth to a boy named Nicholas Tito. She told Nancy that she had called the baby after Lenin and Marshal Tito to annoy her parents. She never changed.

For Debo the time following the outbreak of war was miserable. The rescue of Unity from Europe had been traumatic for her but what made her even more unhappy was Unity's subsequent dislike of her. This led to a very unpleasant atmosphere at Old Mill Cottage where Sydney, Unity and Debo were all cooped up together, with Unity usually venting her bouts of rage on her youngest sister. 'Muv and Bobo are getting awfully on my nerves. I must go away soon, I think,' she wrote to Jessica in 1940. However, in April 1941 Debo became engaged to Lord Andrew Cavendish and they were married the following month, both aged 21. She followed him round to the various training grounds to which he was posted, but when he was sent to Italy with the Coldstream Guards, she went to live on the Derbyshire estate of her in-laws, the Duke and Duchess of Devonshire, where she remained for the rest of the war.

During the war years Debo had three children: a premature son who died almost immediately in November 1941; a daughter, Emma, born safely in 1943; and a son, Peregrine, always known as Stoker, the following year, three weeks before Jessica's son Nicholas. Although they didn't know this at the time, Stoker was to be the future Duke of Devonshire.

When they married there was no hint that Andrew would inherit the title. His elder brother, Billy Hartington, had been groomed for the job and was expected to succeed eventually. Billy was engaged to and later married Kathleen 'Kick' Kennedy, sister of the future US president; this was in spite of opposition from both sets of parents, but especially the Kennedys, because they were Catholics and the Devonshires were staunchly Protestant. They finally married in 1944 and five weeks later Billy was killed fighting in Belgium. As with David during the previous war, Andrew found himself next in line to the family title.

In spite of his support for Nazi Germany, in 1942 Tom joined the Rifle Brigade and fought in North Africa and Italy. As with everything else he ever did, he acquitted himself well and in 1944 he returned to England for a course at the Staff College. He then asked to be sent to Burma as he did not want to have to kill Germans during the Allied occupation of Germany, which clearly was going to take place. Once in Burma he requested a transfer from Staff to a fighting battalion. On 24 March he was leading a force against a group of Japanese armed with machine guns. He was severely wounded and died six days later. He is buried in the military cemetery near Rangoon.

For the sisters it was the greatest tragedy they had ever had to face. Tom was the only one who was always on 'speakers' with all the others; they loved him dearly and remembered with great affection the times when they had made him 'blither' in church, when he had saved them from unwanted partners at debutante dances and introduced them to his much more interesting friends. In all that had happened he was never censorious, keeping in touch with Diana and Mosley yet seeing Jessica and Esmond off to America. He visited Unity and Sydney as often as he could – Unity was always at her best with him – and he spent much of his final leave with Nancy. The fact that he had come unscathed through the greatest part of the war and was the last person they felt would not survive made his death even harder to bear.

For David and Sydney, whose marriage had fallen apart because of their irreconcilable differences in relation to Nazi Germany and Hitler, the death of Tom, their only and much-loved son and heir, must have seemed like the end of the world.

Ten

Pam's War and its Aftermath

There were many times during her life when Pam came to the rescue of her sisters, but none was more heroic than when she took in Diana and Oswald Mosley's two tiny children when their parents were imprisoned during the early years of the war. Urged on by Derek, Pam had 11-week-old Max and 18-month-old Alexander, together with Nanny Higgs, to live at Rignell for almost two years. While Derek was stationed at Middle Wallop he would sometimes pick up Jonathan and Desmond Guinness, Diana's two sons by her first marriage, from their prep. school near Oxford and take them to Rignell for the weekend.

In times of ever-increasing rationing and austerity, with staff leaving to work for the war effort, it was no mean feat for Pam and Derek to help out with Diana's four boys, especially as they had no children of their own. Much later in life, in a letter to Diana, Pam admitted that she really didn't like small children much and felt that she might not have been as kind as she might have been to the boys. Jonathan remembers that she was kind but not affectionate like his mother. Although, in Diana's view, it was a pity that it wasn't possible for the boys to go to Sydney – whose time was completely taken up caring for Unity – it says even more for Pam's courageous spirit that she took on such an enormous task which she couldn't fully enjoy.

There is no hint of these feelings in any of the letters that she wrote to Diana in Holloway prison, where she visited regularly, in spite of the bombing and petrol rationing, taking with her fresh vegetables and eggs from Rignell. She tells her sister how Max – who was still being breast-fed when his mother was imprisoned – was now getting milk from an Ayrshire herd in the village, which is the very best he could have: the milk was not only Tuberculin Tested but also Attested. In the same letter she says that Alexander is having a scarlet woolly coat knitted by Nanny Higgs, as well as the blue one which 'looks lovely', but says, rather significantly, that she teases Nanny who thinks that she pays more attention to the dogs than the babies. Later she writes: 'Both Alexander and Max are extremely well. Apparently Alexander was heard calling this last night when he was meant to be going to sleep, "Trude, Trude, dogs, dogs, dogs!" and as far as he could he was copying my voice. Isn't that extra tum? [a word for sweet invented by Pam and Derek].' She goes on to say: 'I do wish you could have them. I always feel so awful when I can see as much as I like of them and you are unable to do so.'

Sydney, who heroically visited every week, was much preoccupied with the care of Unity; Deborah had recently married and was following her soldier husband, Lord Andrew Cavendish, to different training grounds around the country; Jessica was in America and, because of their very different ideologies, was not in contact with Diana; while Nancy had played a significant part in getting Diana imprisoned, informing MI5 of what she considered to be her sister's unpatriotic behaviour, mainly based on Diana's frequent visits to Germany immediately before the war. In this she was joined by Diana's former father-in-law, Lord Moyne, and Mosley's former sister-in-law, Irene Ravensdale. Apart from their mother, only Pam, in her quiet, courageous way, was able and willing to give regular support to Diana.

In fact, it was no thanks to Nancy, so often a thorn in Pam's flesh, that she and Derek were able to have the boys at Rignell at all. Nancy,

Family group in 1912. Left to right: Nancy, David, Tom, Diana, Sydney and Pam – with dogs. (Copyright the Mitford Archive 2011)

The family with animals *c.* 1915. Left to right: Nancy, Tom, Diana, Unity (on pony), Sydney and Pam. (Copyright the Mitford Archive 2011)

The family continues to grow: Nancy, Pam, Tom, Diana, Unity and Jessica *c*. 1918. Pam is standing awkwardly on her right leg which had been affected by polio. (Copyright the Mitford Archive 2011)

Astall in 1922 when the family was complete. Pam is sat between Tom and David. (Copyright the Mitford Archive 2011)

Jessica, Nancy, Diana, Unity and Pam in 1935. (Copyright the Mitford Archive 2011)

1967. Debo, Nancy, Pam, Diana and Debo's eldest daughter Emma at the wedding party of Debo's son Peregrine, known as Stoker, now the Duke of Devonshire. (Copyright the Mitford Archive 2011)

Pam (third from right) enjoying the Chatsworth Game Fair in the 1980s with her close friend Margaret Budd (on her left). The Duke and Duchess of Devonshire are on the left of the picture. (Photograph courtesy of William Cooper and the executors of Margaret Budd's estate)

Animal lover Pam in conversation with a dog at the home of a friend in the 1980s. (Photograph courtesy of William Cooper and the executors of Margaret Budd's estate)

Pam's gravestone in Swinbrook churchyard. The inscription reads 'a valiant heart'. (Photograph by Christopher Fear)

Woodfield House at Caudle Green in Gloucestershire where Pam spent a contented old age. (Photograph by Christopher Fear)

The 'secret door' into Pam's vegetable garden at Woodfield House. It was designed and made for her by Philip St Pier. (Photograph by Christopher Fear)

Swinbrook church which the Mitford family attended as children and where most of them are buried. Tom's name appears on the war memorial. (Photograph by Christopher Fear)

Asthall Manor, the house which the Mitford family really loved and hated leaving. (Photograph by Christopher Fear)

Pam in a rather serious moment, sitting beside her pale blue Rayburn in her kitchen at Woodfield House. The cabbage is real, the pig's head, in this instance, is a china one. (Photograph courtesy of William Cooper)

Pamela in the early 1930s. In terms of looks she was a close rival to her sister Diana.
(Copyright the Mitford Archive 2011)

presumably feeling she was doing her patriotic duty, told a MI5 officer that Pam and Derek were 'fanatically anti-Semitic, anti-democratic and defeatist'. She also wrote to a friend at the end of 1940 stating that they 'talk such fascism that the whole town is speculating how they manage to stay out [of prison]'. According to Pam's great friend Margaret Budd, who knew Pam during the war and for the rest of her life, she was completely non-political and would never have had such views, let alone expressed them publicly. The most likely explanation for Nancy's statement is that Derek was teasing her by saying that Germany would win the war and that England deserved to lose it and that Pam nodded her agreement. Derek was prone to winding people up but it is hard to believe that this war hero was defeatist, and although he did not particularly like Jews his closest colleague and friend, Heinrich Kuhn, with whom he worked at the Clarendon Laboratory before the war, was a Jewish refugee from Nazi Germany.

In the end, common sense prevailed and the Jacksons were left alone, which was just as well because when the Mosleys were eventually released from prison in November 1943, it was Pam, urged on by Derek, who gave them a temporary home at Rignell. Derek must have known how difficult the situation would become since he was involved in top-secret scientific work with the Telecommunications Research Establishment; but he liked the Mosleys and he was always a loyal friend and a disregarder of authority.

Derek obtained overnight leave so that he could greet the Mosleys on their arrival at Rignell and they were treated to a feast laid on by Pam and attended by Sydney and Debo. For a few days they were able to enjoy the luxury of being looked after by Pam and having nourishing food for the first time in three years; but this was not to last. Within days the press discovered their whereabouts and kept the house under constant surveillance, waiting for the Mosleys to make an appearance. In fact, Pam was the only one they ever saw when she took her dogs for a walk, often after dark, through ploughed fields covered in snow and wearing her wellington boots – she knew that the lightly shod reporters would never follow her over such terrain. On 28 November Diana wrote to Nancy (of whose betrayal she had no idea): 'Woman is being simply too killing, we are besieged by hordes of pressmen and photographers and every now and then she rushes out and says, "I dislike you intensely," or when photo-ed, "You foul man." She doesn't in the least realise what a wonder-working woman she is being.'

In spite of Pam's efforts, the *Daily Express* reported that the house was being guarded by dogs (the dachshunds) and that an air of menace surrounded it:

> Night time in the park gives the house an eerie gloom, with the wind howling in the fir trees, the dogs whining plaintively and the horses neighing at the approach of footsteps ... The secret of Mrs Jackson's visitors has been well kept by the villagers of the neighbouring hamlets round the estate, where Squadron Leader Jackson was 'the squire' before war broke out.

Although Squadron Leader Jackson was highly entertained by such wholly inaccurate reports, feelings against Mosley by a nation at war were extremely inflammatory and soon Derek was forbidden by Home Secretary Herbert Morrison to return to Rignell until the Mosleys had left. Derek was furious and told Morrison exactly what he thought of a man who had been a conscientious objector in the First World War and saw fit to tell a much-decorated RAF officer who he could or could not entertain at his home. There is no record of this interview and Derek's language can only be imagined. In any case, Derek's secret work was incomprehensible to anyone not a physicist.

Diana and Mosley had to go. Lady Redesdale found a home for them to rent at The Shaven Crown, a partly deserted inn at nearby Shipton-under-Wychwood, and for the first time since 1939 Diana, Mosley and Diana's four boys were together for Christmas Day. They spent the day with Lady Redesdale and Unity, all crammed into the tiny dining room of Old Mill Cottage at Swinbrook where, due to the lack of turkeys and geese, they ate 'a large, enormous chicken which was almost as good'.

When the war ended Derek became increasingly disillusioned with post-war Great Britain and the tremendous tax burden which the new Labour government levied on people as wealthy as him. He was offered the post of Professor of Spectroscopy at Oxford – and was made a Fellow of the Royal Society – but he and Pam decided to settle in Ireland where taxes were not so high and where he could resume his love affair with horses, racing and hunting.

Derek was not an ungenerous man – he made grants to Oxford University for the benefit of the Clarendon Laboratory and made a substantial contribution towards the installation of a spectroscope at the Oxford Observatory. His spat with Herbert Morrison – now number two in the Atlee government – over the Mosleys did nothing to make him want to stay in England. The last straw was the Inland Revenue's attempt to make his wartime earnings subject to surtax, when he had intended to donate the money to a trust for RAF widows. He declared his intention to leave England for good.

As well as the advantageous tax laws, it was a visit to Lismore Castle in County Waterford, where Derek and Pam stayed with Debo and her husband Andrew, which finally persuaded Derek to choose Ireland as his home. Lismore is a fairytale castle and one of the great sights of that part of the world. Derek was seduced by the good weather and the prospect of endless hunting and racing in this Land of the Horse. It must have been hard for Pam to leave her native Oxfordshire but, presumably, in her usual way, she fell in with Derek's plans. In fact, it was she who was happiest in Ireland while Derek in the end became bored.

To start with, however, it seemed like a good decision. Derek and Pam bought a more modest castle called Tullamaine, in County Tipperary, and Pam was delighted to be close to Debo when she was at Lismore. Tullamaine was a Gothic-style castle with plenty of stabling built in the 1830s in the heart of Tipperary Hunt country. The nearest town was called Fethard (pronounced feathered) and Pam, the poultry lover, would tell her friends that she now lived 'in a Fethard world'. She settled in quickly, became involved in village life, loved the local countryside and, as always, was entirely happy surrounded by horses, dogs and chickens.

At first, Derek also enjoyed life in Ireland. He hunted regularly, riding like a jockey with short stirrups and, endearingly, always giving his horse a hug at the end of the day. He was granted a trainer's licence and rode as an amateur jockey. But it wasn't enough for this brilliant, restless man. He went on lecture tours to America, but he refused to be enticed back to Oxford by Lord Cherwell, his old boss, and he became bored with Irish rural life; he enjoyed little success as a trainer and took scant interest in local affairs. In spite of Pam's wifely qualities, excellent culinary skills, their still-shared love of horses and dogs and the frequent company of Pam's young nephew, Desmond Guinness, who was a lively riding and racing companion, he began to spend time in Dublin, England and sometimes America. As well as venting his anger and frustration on Pam, who certainly did not deserve it, he began to be unfaithful, which she didn't deserve either.

She seemed to accept his behaviour, probably believing that if it had not been for the war he might well have left her by now. Even so, when he announced to her his intention of marrying Janetta Kee – already twice married and with a child by another man, but more sharp-witted, intellectual and politically aware than Pam – she was bitterly hurt. She had lost her only brother, Tom, right at the end of the war, and Unity had died of meningitis in 1948; now Derek was leaving her after fourteen years of marriage. They were divorced in 1951.

Pam stayed on at Tullamaine after Derek left and was kept busy by visits from her family, particularly the Mosleys who lived with her while they too looked for a home in Ireland, eventually buying an old bishop's palace in County Galway. Her companion of the time was a Swiss riding teacher called Giuditta Tommasi whom Pam had met while she was teaching equestrian skills to the two Mosley boys.

Pam was then faced with the dilemma of whether to move to Switzerland with Giuditta or to Germany to be near her friend Rudi von Simolin. She and Rudi had met when Pam had travelled to Germany with her mother at the end of the war to thank her for visiting Unity every day when she was in hospital. Pam and Rudi became lifelong friends, though in the end, Pam chose to move to Switzerland with Giuditta, having also bought a house in the Cotswold village of Caudle Green.

Eleven

Post-War: A Time for Moving On

Pam and Derek were not the only ones to move from England after the war. It had been such a traumatic time for the family that new starts were necessary. Nancy's move to France was the most permanent. Having gone there at the end of the war ostensibly to do business for Heywood Hill's bookshop but really to be near her beloved Colonel, she had such success with her novel *The Pursuit of Love* that she lived in Paris and later in Versailles for the rest of her life. Initially she lived in small hotels or rented flats on the Left Bank, near to the Colonel, and finally settled at 7 rue Monsieur where she remained until 1966. There she was looked after by her devoted maid Marie and shared the flat with a ginger and white cat given to her by Diana and a white hen. The cat and the hen never bothered one another.

Her happiness at being financially independent at last was marred by the fact that although she was in love with the Colonel for the rest of her life, his passion for her was largely over by the time she came to live in Paris. They remained close lifelong friends but she had to share him with other women and also with General de Gaulle, in whose government he served, and make the most of the time they spent together. She now had plenty of money, however, and was able to enjoy her life in Paris and indulge her passion for haute couture, being one of the first women to wear Christian Dior's 'New Look' with its long elegant skirts and fitted waists which so suited her slim figure and were the opposite of the short skirts and wide shoulders of wartime 'fashion'.

As soon as she had a settled home, Nancy started work on *Love in a Cold Climate*, the sequel to *The Pursuit of Love*. The same characters appear but they are no longer centre stage, this position being given to the grand and wealthy Montdores and – a real departure from the novels of the time – the colourful and eccentric homosexual Cedric. The 'I' of the novel is still Fanny, now married to an Oxford don, giving Nancy the opportunity to use her sharp wit against the rarefied world of academia. Fanny and her family take the central role in a further sequel, *Don't Tell Alfred*, published in 1960, in which Fanny's husband is unexpectedly made British ambassador to Paris. The book did not enjoy the success of the first two, but is equally enjoyable and still very funny. In it Nancy draws on her friendship with Duff and Diana Cooper whom she visited often during her early days in Paris, when Duff was British ambassador and Diana a superb hostess. In between these two novels she wrote *The Blessing* – an account of a small child playing his estranged parents off against the other. All ends happily – and the characters appear again, very much married, in *Don't Tell Alfred*.

Nancy also adapted and translated *The Little Hut*, a farce by André Roussin, which had a very successful British tour and a good London run. In contrast, she began to write historical biographies, starting with *Madame de Pompadour* and following it with *Voltaire in Love*. Although these initially received mixed reviews, Nancy, who stopped writing novels in 1960, became respected as a biographer, going on to write *The Sun King*, the life of Louis XIV, and finishing *Frederick the Great* not long before she died.

Apart from the success of these books, Nancy is best remembered for her send-up of class snobbery which first appeared in the magazine *Encounter* in November 1955. Entitled 'U and Non-U' it distinguishes between upper- and non-upper-class language and was originally written with linguistics professor Alan Ross of Birmingham University. So popular was this piece that *Encounter* went into a reprint (unheard of for an intellectual monthly magazine) and the article was turned into a slim volume entitled *Noblesse Oblige*. It was the subject of John Betjeman's poem 'How to get on in Society', and to this day there are those who still can't decide whether to call a toilet a lavatory – or vice versa, a lounge a drawing room, or if a serviette is really a table napkin.

The Mosley family, in contrast to Nancy, were going nowhere after the war as their passports were still confiscated. They had moved to Crowood in Wiltshire because the house had farmland attached to it and it gave Mosley something with which to occupy his time. Mosley was only 49 when the war ended and he needed something more to do with his undoubted energies than live the life of a country gentleman – but what? The name Mosley was hated in post-war as well as wartime England, to the extent that very few schools would accept Alex and Max, who ended up being educated by a tutor. Diana realised very soon that there was little chance of her husband ever getting back into politics but she made it her life's work to encourage him to think that he might do so. His first course was to champion a united Europe which would be a bastion against communism, and in this he was well ahead of his time, but first he had to get his views aired in public. He started the monthly *Mosley Newsletter*, followed by the weekly *Union*, later called *Action*. He founded a new party called the Union Movement but it was difficult to hire a hall once the owners learnt his name. He did actually stand for Parliament in 1959 and 1966 but each time lost his deposit. More successful was the Mosleys' founding of a monthly intellectual magazine, *The European*, which Diana edited between 1953 and 1959. It never made money and eventually Mosley closed it down, but it had attracted some formidable right-wing writers and, more importantly, it had illustrated that Diana too had the literary flair inherited from both her grandfathers.

By 1947 the Mosleys were still having their request for passports turned down. To get around this Mosley bought a 60-ton ketch, the *Alianora*, and arranged with his contacts in Franco's Spain and

Salazar's Portugal that they would accept him and his family without passports. Just as they were about to sail in 1949 their passports were granted, but they kept to their plans and spent the summer sailing in the Mediterranean with Alex and Max.

This episode and the loss of a tax case convinced Mosley in 1950 that it would be a good idea to emigrate; the death of Diana's dear and loyal friend, the aesthete Lord Berners (on whom Nancy had based the character of Lord Merlin in *The Pursuit of Love* and *Love in a Cold Climate*), removed one of the only obstacles which would have persuaded her to stay. Pam and Derek had already established themselves at Tullamaine Castle, and Debo and Andrew spent time at their Irish property, Lismore Castle. In 1951 Mosley sold Crowood and bought Clonfert Palace in east Galway and the Temple de la Gloire at Orsay outside Paris. Clonfert and most of its contents were burnt down two years later and thereafter the Mosleys made their home at Orsay, which meant that Nancy and Diana saw each other often. Nancy and Mosley did not get on but years of being polite to one another for Diana's sake eventually established a sort of friendship. Strangely, in view of their very differing political opinions, Mosley and the Colonel got on well, possibly because Mosley never got involved in French politics as he did in Spain, Italy and Germany.

The lives of Diana and Nancy came to be opposites of one another. Diana's personal life was near perfect: she lived for Mosley and he for her and she had four healthy sons. But their political lives were doomed to disappointment because there was no way that Mosley would ever establish a serious following for his views once fascism had become so reviled in Europe. Nancy, on the other hand, had achieved fame and fortune through her writing but her personal life was doomed to childlessness and disappointment. After many years of refusing to give her a divorce, she and Peter finally parted for good in 1958, but even this did not improve her situation with the Colonel who married someone else in the mid-1960s.

Before the end of the war Sydney and Unity were also on the move, spending much of their time on the Scottish island of Inch Kenneth, since they were no longer thought to be a security risk. David, after

Unity was reunited with the family and feeling that he could no longer live with Sydney when the two had such opposing political views, spent half of the year on Inch Kenneth and the other half at the family's London home in Rutland Gate. His constant companion for the rest of his life was Margaret Wright who had been assistant parlour maid at Rutland Gate and was also a trained nurse. Most of the family found her bossy and possessive and Debo really disliked her, but she loyally looked after David who had aged prematurely, largely due to the many family dramas and tragedies which had beset him. After five years of living between two places, he and Margaret went to live in Redesdale Cottage in Northumberland and Sydney and Unity divided their time between Inch Kenneth and Swinbrook.

It was on Inch Kenneth, in 1948, that Unity contracted meningitis, probably from the bullet wound in her head. The weather was bad so there was a delay in getting her to hospital in Oban, where she died on 28 May. David travelled to Oban to be with Sydney, and Unity was later buried at Swinbrook at a service attended by all her sisters except for Jessica and at which the hymns were those that Unity had previously chosen. When Jessica heard of Unity's death she declared that for her, the old Unity had died when she realised they couldn't be friends any more, but Dinky later reported that her mother was heartbroken by the news. On Unity's now-weathered gravestone it is still possible to read the inscription put there by Sydney: 'Say Not the Struggle Naught Availeth' – a line from Winston Churchill's favourite poem during the war.

Earlier that year Sydney had made the longest journey of her life when she flew to San Francisco to see Jessica and her family. She was 68 and to fly to the other side of the world in the late 1940s must have taken some courage, even though air travel had progressed enormously since Pam and Derek flew across the Atlantic shortly before the war. But Sydney was her father's daughter and travel was in her bones.

The visit had come about because in January 1948 Dinky had written a Christmas thank-you letter to her grandmother asking her to come and stay. Sydney decided to grasp the nettle and make peace with Jessica with whom she had kept in touch over all the difficult years. Jessica had given birth to a second son, Benjy, a few months before and Sydney was keen to meet her American grandchildren and also Bob. Things were not easy at first as the two women tried to negotiate a relationship after all the things that had divided them, but Sydney was determined that the visit should be a success, and it was. Sydney loved the children, taught Dinky to knit and christened Nicholas 'My little Okay' because he answered 'Okay' to everything. She got on well with Bob and his mother Aranka and with all their friends. 'I really rather adored her,' admitted Jessica at the end of the visit. Debo visited the Treuhafts in 1950 when, to Jessica's disappointment, some of her communist friends were rather deferential to the duchess.

Jessica and Bob continued to work for the Civil Rights Movement and the Communist Party, although Jessica, always the tease, found some of the comrades rather self-righteous and dull. Bob's legal business was busy but did not make much money since most of his clients were poor black Americans.

Early in 1955 yet another tragedy engulfed Jessica when Nicholas was killed by a bus while on his paper round. The whole family was devastated, especially Dinky, who was in charge of her brothers while her parents were at work and held herself responsible. Bob and Jessica were so distraught that they could not even comfort one another and Nicholas was never talked about after that. Sydney, who knew what it was like to lose a son, wrote to Jessica mourning the death of her 'little Okay'. For Jessica it was the fifth loss of someone she loved dearly – baby Julia, Esmond, Tom, Unity and now her beloved eldest son.

Later that year, Jessica and her family visited Europe in spite of an attempt by the US government not to issue passports. They visited Inch Kenneth and then went to Edensor, near Chatsworth, where Debo and her family were then living. The visit did not go smoothly and Jessica admitted that she was 'not a good guest'. They went from England to Hungary where Bob's family had come from and then to Paris to visit Nancy, who had taken fright at the thought of this all-American family trashing her precious flat and fled to Chatsworth to stay with Debo. She did return to Paris and the visit was a success, with Jessica and Nancy chatting together as in the old days while never actually divulging to one another their innermost thoughts. Jessica did not see Diana, either then or on other family visits, until Nancy was dying, but she saw Pam in London.

Jessica and Bob remained sympathetic to the communist cause but chose to leave the party, feeling that they could do more good as non-communists in a country where left-wing politics were viewed as a crime. Before this Jessica, finding the communist language and jargon so impenetrable, wrote a pamphlet entitled 'Lifeitselfmanship', or 'How to become a Precisely Because Man', gently poking fun at the leaden language used by party officials. Though frowned upon by the party leadership, the pamphlet was a great success and showed that many communists were actually able to laugh at themselves.

Encouraged by the success of 'Lifeitselfmanship', Jessica produced *Hons and Rebels*, an account of her childhood as she saw it, which was published in 1960. The reading public was already familiar with the Mitford family through Nancy's novels, but *Hons and Rebels* was altogether sharper, altogether more 'Jessica', and tended to laugh at the family rather than with them. It became an instant success both in America and Britain, making Jessica a recognised author and per-sonality; it meant that she could then spend the rest of her life as a writer and journalist. The book was not popular within the family, however, as it is full of inaccuracies or perceived inaccuracies, many of them quite cruel. Sydney, older and wiser than the others, was kinder, although she also disliked much of it, saying that she was pleasantly surprised that the book was not more furious against everyone.

David did not live to see its publication. He had died in 1958, a broken man and older than his years. Diana, Debo and Sydney had been with him a few days previously, for his 80th birthday, and all the sisters were at his funeral, except Jessica whom he also left out of his will. This was partly because of her unsuccessful attempt in the 1940s to sell her share of Inch Kenneth (David had made the island over to Tom, after whose death it passed to his sisters) to the Communist Party. Nancy felt that Jessica had been unfairly treated in the will and gave her share of the island to her. In the end Jessica, after receiving a legacy from Esmond's family, bought the whole island and signed it over to Sydney for her lifetime.

Debo did not move far after the war, only from The Rookery, on the Chatsworth estate, to Edensor House in the nearest village to Chatsworth. Chatsworth House, the traditional seat of the Devonshire family, had been taken over by Penrhos College, a girls' boarding school, during the war and bore the signs of being inhabited by schoolgirls for seven years. The present Duke and Duchess had never considered living there but in 1949, after considerable renovation, the gardens and some of the staterooms were reopened to the public.

Andrew stood for Parliament as a Conservative in 1945, at the time of the great Atlee landslide, and although Debo had no interest in politics (like Pam), she supported him by going canvassing with him; she vowed she would never do so again, however, after being tripped up, spat on and nearly having their car overturned. 'They like 'im, but they say booger 'is party,' was one observer's comment. Andrew stood again in 1950 (without Debo's help) but was again unsuccessful.

In 1946 Andrew's father made over the estate to him in order to avoid the crippling death duties levied by the Labour government. He had to live for five years after the transfer to comply with the inheritance laws and as he was only 51 and in good health, this seemed a good move. But in November 1950 the duke died of a heart attack, aged 55, while chopping wood on his estate near Eastbourne. It was fourteen weeks short of the statutory five years and death duties of 80 per cent were now due on the estate, which looked as if it would have to be broken up and many of its treasures sold. Andrew and Debo were not prepared to let this happen without a fight. Although Debo is always credited with saving Chatsworth, she is the first to admit that it was Andrew's shrewd sale of land, works of art and beautiful Hardwick Hall – which had been in the Cavendish family for fifteen generations and was sold to the National Trust – which saved Chatsworth from being gobbled up by the Inland Revenue. Even so, it took seventeen years of negotiations and the final payment was not made until 1974.

In the mid-1950s the family moved into the house in order to open it to the public and make it a paying concern. Debo decided that she would undertake the decoration herself, as Sydney had always done, but it was a huge project as the house had 175 rooms, 24 bathrooms, 21 kitchens and 17 staircases, making Batsford with its five staircases look like a country cottage. Nevertheless she succeeded. 'Nobody could have done it as well,' wrote Nancy in a letter to Diana. Praise indeed.

It was not all work and no play, however, for Andrew and Debo were able to escape at intervals from their new responsibilities and the austerity of post-war England by visiting the south of France and Italy. Debo also had holidays with her friend Prince Aly Khan at his fabulous villa in France, where she mixed with famous film stars. But there was sadness, too, for after the birth of Stoker in 1944 she lost three babies, before Sophia was safely delivered in 1957. As the sister who was closest to David and shared his interests, she must have felt his death the following year very keenly; also that of Unity, in spite of their differences in later years. There was yet another tragedy for Debo in the same year that Unity died: Kathleen 'Kick' Kennedy, widow of Andrew's elder brother Billy, sister of future American president Jack and Debo's close friend from debutante days, was killed in an air crash. Kick had fallen in love again but with a married man. They were on their way to Cannes for the weekend when they flew into a storm and the plane crashed with no survivors. Rose Kennedy, who had threatened to disown her if she married a divorced man, declared that it was God saying 'no' to Kick. Debo organised her funeral and she is buried at Edensor where Debo has tended her grave ever since.

The period from the end of the war until the swinging sixties was not as traumatic for the Mitford family as what had gone before, despite the loss of Unity, Nicholas Treuhaft and David. There were many positives: Nancy was a popular published writer and Jessica was on her way to being the same. The Mosleys' marriage was on a firmer footing than ever before and Pam was making a new life for herself after her divorce from Derek. Chatsworth would eventually be saved for the nation, Sydney was reconciled with Jessica and was enjoying a rather quieter life on her much-loved Inch Kenneth. At last the family seemed, in Grandfather Bowles's language, to be sailing into calmer waters.

Twelve

After Derek

After Derek left, Pam was still very much immersed in Irish life, so much so that Diana and Debo believed she had far too much to do while she stayed at Tullamaine. And they had cause to worry, if a previously unpublished letter from Pam to Debo written in January 1957, a year before Tullamaine was sold, is anything to go by:

I *was* pleased to hear from you. My life is just one long rush and if I start the morning in gumboots I somehow never have time to change them till the evening! Today was hectic and it was the day of Alice Daly my charming daily! I have two, one is super, Bridie, and she comes four times a week, the other is old Alice Daly and although she polishes the floors better than anyone else she is such an effort and somehow I always find she almost makes more work than she does!

Anyway today the Hounds met a mile away so what with having to ride one horse to the meet, cadge a lift home, cook a meal for Alice, rush down to the Lodge and see how it was getting on in readiness for the Hungarian refugees, then finish getting Alice's lunch, then rushing off with the dogs to see the men who are cutting larch trees, then back to find someone ringing at the front door with a parcel of things to help with the furnishing of the cottage for the refugees, then mixing the horses' mash, then rushing to the Fethard World with urgent letters for the Post, ending with a call at McCarthy's Hotel and drinks with friends.

Now you know what a normal day is like for me and, yes, Derek agrees it would be better to sell this so if you know anyone who would like it do send them to have a look. I would really be so much more comfortable in something smaller and really England would be better as this is so far from everyone and everything.

How lovely it would be if you and I could share a life as I would love to spend half a day sometimes in bed and you might like to do some of my rushing for me.

Pam continued to live at Tullamaine even after it was sold early in 1956, since the buyer did not want to live in the house. She and Giuditta Tommasi stayed there as tenants until 1960 when they moved briefly to Woodfield House in Caudle Green in the Cotswolds, which Pam had bought with her proceeds of the sale. She had not been very happy at Tullamaine since Derek had left – it was too full of memories – but she was unsure what she wanted to do next or where she wanted to live. Her plan was to let Woodfield until such time as she decided to live in England again.

Two events which were added to the Mitford family sagas emerge from the time Pam spent at Tullamaine after Derek left. While she was a tenant there she persuaded her landlord to install a new electricity system and he sent along a team of workmen to rewire the house. Then she asked him to provide a cow as she had no milk for their tea and again he duly obliged, sending a splendid cow in a lorry from Cork, 70 miles away. As the men used only a small amount of milk each day Pam bought four piglets and reared them on some of the remainder, sending the rest to the local creamery. She then received a cheque for £10 from the creamery, but when a friend suggested that she should reimburse the landlord, she was indignant. 'Oh, no!' she shrieked in horror. 'After all, MY gardener milks the cow! And but for me the workmen would have had to BUY milk in the Fethard World!'

'So,' wrote Diana in a letter to Debo, 'she keeps the cheque and the pigs – and the workmen are only there because *she* insisted. I thought we should die of laughter as the story unfolded. Isn't she WONDAIR?'

When Pam finally left Tullamaine she held a sale of her belongings. Glasses which she had bought at the local Woolworth's – where they could still be bought – fetched four times their retail price and she included in the sale large jars of eggs which had been stored in brine the year before. Diana and Debo teased her, saying that the eggs would have gone bad and would explode at intervals during the sale (they didn't), but she took no notice and announced several times during proceedings in a loud voice: 'Nothing leaves this house until it is paid for.' This story is reminiscent of a previous occasion, this time when Pam and Derek were leaving Rignell. They invited the Mosleys to see if they wanted to buy anything from the house and during the evening Derek, becoming somewhat drunk and very sentimental, was heard by Pam to say to her sister: 'Darling Diana, you mustn't pay a penny for anything.'

'Nothing leaves this house until she pays,' said Pam in great indignation.

During the time Pam spent in the Cotswolds before moving to Switzerland, Giuditta, who had accompanied her to England, trained her horse at Sudgrove House, the home of former Olympic show-jumping rider Pat Smythe. Pat was soon to marry Swiss businessman Sam Koechlin, also an international showjumper. Local farmer Malcolm Whitaker remembers Giuditta riding over to his farm in nearby Syde to ask if she could gallop her horse across his fields. Her ready smile and attractive manner always brightened his day – and he never refused her request. He felt that she came to ride on the farm partly because she very much enjoyed speaking German to his great friend Rudi Lomberg, a former German officer who had been taken prisoner during the war and chosen to stay in England. He worked with Malcolm on the farm and enjoyed these encounters with Giuditta as much as she did.

Due to her family's friendship with Sam, a young Swiss girl, Margrit Kottmann, came to work on the farm at Sudgrove House for a year as part of her training. There she met Giuditta who took her home to

Woodfield to meet Pam. This was the start of a friendship which provided a link between Switzerland and the Cotswolds and lasted until Pam's death, since Margrit married George Powell, a local farmer, and made her home near Cheltenham. They had many meals with Pam at Caudle Green and enjoyed her excellent cooking, which Margrit remembers as being simple but very imaginative.

> She once gave us mince flavoured with lemon and herbs but not with tomato, which was very unusual but tasted delicious and I remember her teaching my mother how to add curry powder to salad dressing to make it more tasty and also to add two to three dashes of Worcestershire sauce to Yorkshire pudding batter to give it extra zest.

George and Margrit still have in their garden plants which Pam gave them to remind them of her friendship. One of these is sorrel and Margrit still makes sorrel soup from Pam's recipe (see Appendix).

When living in Switzerland Pam became friendly with Margrit's parents who lived in the Jura mountains, and Margrit and her family visited Pam at her house in Grüningen, the tiny, low-lying village near Zurich where she had finally chosen to live. Years later, after Pam had left Switzerland, Giuditta, who had stayed on in the house, died suddenly from an asthma attack; it was Margrit's son, Dan, and his friend Chris Thring who drove from Gloucestershire to Grüningen in an ancient van to bring back some furniture which Pam had left there. She had been quoted a price by a local removal firm which she was not prepared to pay!

The house in Grüningen was set amid picture-book scenery and was what Debo described as 'an odd little house with a ladder to the bedrooms' – not, you might think, a suitable staircase for someone with a weak leg but, 'I've insured myself against accidents hurrying down to answer the telephone,' Pam assured Diana. Inside, Pam's house had a 'vast china stove fed from the kitchen with wood', which added to the warm and welcoming atmosphere always associated with her homes; the fact that all the houses in the village had very low doorways must have added to the feeling of cosiness inside.

The relationship between Pam and Giuditta has caused speculation, though not as much as it would if they were sharing a home today. Jessica was convinced it was a lesbian relationship and during a visit to England in 1955 wrote home to her husband Bob that her sister had become a 'you-know-what-bian'. But Jessica's descriptions of family members are notoriously inaccurate – her book *Hons and Rebels*, entertaining though it is, caused a great furore among the family due to some of the things she had said about them, which may have been as she saw them but were not entirely true. Diana, characteristically, was kinder about Pam: 'I don't know if they were lovers but it really was a kind of marriage'; while Diana's son Jonathan Guinness is of the opinion that the exact relationship was not important – Pam had found a good companion to share her life with at a time when she badly needed friends.

Men certainly continued to find her attractive. Those she met in Switzerland couldn't wait to take her out to meals and in 1969 Danish architect and painter Mogens Tvede wanted to marry her ('He saw at a glance that she is the PICK of the Bunch. Clever old Dane,' wrote Nancy to Debo), though this came to nothing. Not long after this – and she was over 60 at the time – she was asked out to lunch at a very expensive Paris restaurant by an old admirer whom she hadn't seen for thirty-five years. She was somewhat apprehensive because she feared she might not recognise him since she could only remember that he was very tall. Sadly, there is no record of the actual meeting – if indeed they ever found one another – but, according to Nancy, Pam threw caution to the winds and went to the restaurant in a taxi. 'She had her hair done yesterday and looks smashing … One can see the eyes from the other end of the passage.' (More than all the others Pam had inherited her father's bright blue eyes.) Even Derek, after they had settled their post-marital differences, made no secret of the fact that he found her very attractive, always paying great attention to her at the family parties to which he was still invited.

Pam got on very well with the Swiss people. She spoke to them in very correct high-class German, but those who spoke English, when they met her in the street, would cry, 'Pamailah, how vonderful to see you!'

'She is absolute monarch of ALL she surveys. She is Queen in Gruningen and receives waves and smiles from every door and window as she pounds along screaming at the Elles [dogs],' wrote Diana to Debo after a visit. The sisters used to tease Pam that she knew all the Gnomes in Zurich and it wasn't far from the truth. 'I worship the Gnomes,' she would say, and she especially enjoyed the way they would click their heels, kiss her hand and ask her out to lunch. In Switzerland she was loved for all the qualities which made her popular wherever she went and her Swiss friends would listen hour on hour while she regaled them with tales of her childhood.

Switzerland was a good centre for Pam to indulge in her love of travel and she often visited Rudi von Simolin in Bavaria, drove to Paris to see Nancy and Diana, and to Chatsworth to stay with Debo. She made many visits to Nancy after she was diagnosed with cancer in 1968. Pam hated staying in Nancy's flat, which she found uncomfortable and claustrophobic, but she went whenever she could because of all the sisters it was she who gave Nancy the most comfort when she was at her worst. In her better moments, Pam would make her laugh, recalling stories of her dogs, her household affairs and Derek's eccentricities during their married life. In 1969 she went with Nancy to Dresden and Potsdam for Nancy to research the life of Frederick the Great, whose biography she was writing. Pam was the ideal companion for the trip, not only because she spoke German fluently, which Nancy did not, but also because, as the journey progressed, Nancy's condition worsened and Pam was there to comfort and reassure her.

Pam had also been invaluable some years earlier, in May 1963, when Lady Redesdale was dying on the island of Inch Kenneth, and Nancy, Pam, Diana and Debo all travelled to the island to look after her. Although they relished being together and were very glad that they could all share in looking after their mother, it was a heart-rending time for them. But the practicalities of life had to go on and Pam was the one who came to the rescue. 'My clothes are all dirty, so I said to Debo, "I'm going to make Woman teach me to wash and I'll stand and look on while she does." Well it worked like a charm and now she's going to teach me to iron,' wrote Nancy to Jessica, in one of her many letters keeping her informed of their mother's deteriorating condition. Needless to say, Pam also did the cooking, which must have raised their spirits at this very difficult time.

Lady Redesdale died on 25 May 1963, aged 83, but long before this her face showed the strain which her family had caused her: Nancy's writing about the family could be very cruel and gave her much pain; Diana's divorce and remarriage were a terrible worry until she realised that Diana was supremely happy with Sir Oswald Mosley; Jessica running away to Spain with her cousin Esmond Romilly was a dreadful shock; and the estrangement from her husband made her very unhappy. None of this, though, could compare with the loss of Unity, whom she looked after until she died, and the death of Tom on active service in Burma in the final year of the war. In spite of all her anxiety, she was always the rock on whom her children depended. That mantle now passed jointly to Pam and Debo, the two daughters who had seldom given her any cause for worry. Debo did her best – and largely succeeded – to smooth over the many differences between the sisters, while Pam used her womanly skills and great kindness and understanding to look after them when they were sick or sad.

When Pam went to live in Switzerland, she took her dachshunds with her, announcing that she would stay there until they died. She told a reporter from a Swiss magazine (to whom she was giving an interview for an article about the Mitford sisters entitled 'Six Black Sheep') that this was not just because of the quarantine regulations which then existed, but because she thought they would like to spend their old age on the Continent. What the reporter thought of this reply can only be a matter of speculation; but she was serious.

The removal of the dachshunds to Switzerland in the first place must have been something of a relief to Debo who, although a real dog-lover herself, had had more than enough of Pam and her dogs after a visit to Chatsworth for Christmas 1960. She describes to Diana how Pam dedicated the whole time to her dogs: cooking 'crank foods' like rice and brown bread, as well as meat, feeding them and taking them out for walks, then repeating these three operations at intervals throughout the day. When the dogs came in muddy from their walks they jumped up on the sofas and she made no attempt to stop them except by speaking very loudly to them, to which they took no notice. Debo bore this recipe for a disastrous Christmas with great fortitude, remarking only that: 'She is herself with knobs on.'

Pam enjoyed her time in Switzerland but eventually she longed to come home and only the two remaining dogs, Hexlie (German for little witch) and Susie, kept her there. She may also have begun to find the Swiss pride in hygiene a little irksome because on one of her visits to England she remarked triumphantly to Margrit and George Powell: 'I'm delighted to hear that they've found salmon in the Thames and there aren't many in the river down there [in Switzerland]. Raise the Union Jack!'

It should be added, however, that Pam's command of the German language, which she had taught herself and made her very comfortable with the Swiss, is yet another indication that she was quite as intelligent as her siblings.

Eventually both dogs shuffled off their canine coil and Pam was able to return to England, after more than twenty years of living in Ireland and 'on the Continent' as she called it. She couldn't wait to get home.

Thirteen

Middle-Aged Mitfords

One of the first big events for Debo in the swinging sixties was the inauguration of President Kennedy in 1961, to which she and Andrew were invited and treated as important guests. This was due to Debo's staunch friendship with 'Kick' Kennedy, the president's sister, who was married to Andrew's elder brother who was killed in Belgium in 1944. When Kennedy was assassinated in November 1963 they were also present at his state funeral.

The death of Sydney in May 1963 shook the Mitford Girls possibly more than they expected, especially Nancy and Jessica, whose portrayal of the family in their writing had been very hurtful to their mother, although she usually tried to conceal her feelings. She had, however, had a furious row with Nancy about a very unsympathetic portrait of her in a little book entitled *The Water Beetle*, published in 1962, and this had not really been resolved.

Sydney, having spent the winter of 1962/63 in London, set off for Inch Kenneth in the spring, accompanied by Madeau Stewart, one of the Mitford cousins, who loved both Sydney and the island and had spent much time there in recent years. Sydney had had Parkinson's disease for some time but she had not let it affect her life. After the journey to the island, however, Madeau was worried about her and called the doctor, who diagnosed her to be in the terminal stages of the disease and deteriorating rapidly. Nancy, Pam, Diana and Debo all came to the island to look after her, with the help of two trained nurses. The sisters kept Jessica up to date by almost daily letters. Sydney died on 25 May, shortly after her 83rd birthday.

It was an agonising time for the sisters as Sydney hovered between life and death, but it was also cathartic since they had time to spend together and to reflect on the mother which some of them had felt to be inadequate but who was really the rock of their extraordinary family. This was the time when gentle, capable Pam took over many of the aspects of caring for Sydney and looking after the others. Sydney, by her own wish, was buried at Swinbrook, next to David, on the first really warm spring day of the year, when Swinbrook looked at its very best.

The same year, Jessica enjoyed enormous success with *The American Way of Death*, a description and attack on the American funeral industry which for years had divested bereaved families of huge sums of money for their loved ones' funerals. The cost of dying, Jessica declared, was rising faster than the cost of living. The book, with which just about every reader could identify and which was savagely funny, was top of the bestseller charts for months and was the book of which Jessica became most proud. Except for *A Fine Old Conflict*, the sequel to *Hons and Rebels*, published in 1977, which again ruffled family feathers, she never quite reached the heights of *The American Way of Death*. (An inexpensive coffin became known as a Mitford, causing hilarity among the sisters.) Her campaign for a fairer world which she had once demonstrated by her actions, she now fought for in her writing, and she was always supported by Bob who helped her with the research. *The Making of a Muckraker*, published in 1979, is a collection of her articles on the subjects about which she felt most strongly, including funerals, prison conditions and civil rights.

Jessica was offered several short-term academic posts, including one at Harvard and another at Yale, and as a lecturer her humour and wit meant that she was very popular with her students. The honorary degree of Doctor of Letters which she received from San Jose

University caused her to write to one of her sisters: 'Wouldn't Muv be amazed to find that Little D [Sydney's pet name for Jessica] has been transformed into D Litt?' The irony of the situation for one who claimed she had been denied a proper education by her parents cannot have been lost on her sisters.

By the 1960s it was obvious to Nancy that her relationship with the Colonel was never again going to be any more than that of a dear friend. She tried not to be jealous when she saw him with other women and to avoid this happening too often she moved to an apartment in Versailles in 1967. Worse was to come. Palewski had always told Nancy that to marry a divorced Protestant (Nancy and Peter had finally divorced in 1958) would harm his political career, but he then married in the mid-1960s a duchess who was also a divorced Protestant. Nancy tried to pretend, even to Diana, that she didn't mind but she was bitterly unhappy, even though she and the Colonel remained friends. Only two years after moving to Versailles, Nancy became ill with what was eventually diagnosed as Hodgkin's disease, a form of leukaemia; this was after many misdiagnoses, numerous tests and treatments which failed to help at all. For much of the time she was in great pain, particularly in her back. An operation to remove a lump, supposedly benign, from the base of her spine did not help for long, though she had a period of remission in which she started the research for her biography of Frederick the Great, travelling to Germany with Pam as interpreter; when the pain gradually returned Pam also acted as her nurse.

Nancy never knew that she had cancer because Pam, Diana and Debo felt that if she was told she would give up. Jessica, as usual (though it was a valid opinion and one which would be unquestioned today), felt that this was wrong because it deprived Nancy of any feeling of urgency about setting her life in order. But Jessica was far away and the others, particularly Pam and Diana, were caring for Nancy so their view prevailed. One good thing which came of Nancy's illness was that for the first time since before the war, Diana and Jessica spent time together when Jessica visited Nancy in Versailles. On the surface they enjoyed friendly chats but never spoke of the events which had divided them and they did not meet again after Nancy's death. She died on 30 June 1973 and it is thought that the last person she recognised was the Colonel, who was one of the few non-family visitors during her last days.

She was cremated in Paris and her ashes buried at Swinbrook, next to Unity. 'Nancy was the brightest star of our youth,' wrote their cousin Joan Farrer to Jessica, who did not attend the funeral but had it described to her by Diana and Debo. Unlucky in love, Nancy was incredibly successful in her career and she had been delighted when, the previous year, she was awarded both the CBE and the Legion of Honour for her contribution to literature.

After fighting the 1959 general election on behalf of his Union Movement, Sir Oswald Mosley stood once again in 1966 but once again was defeated, although he did receive 10 per cent of the vote. He then gave up the leadership of the party but continued to promote a European union both on the Continent and also in Britain. This was not easy because he was still very much the bogey man to the British public – as late as 1962 he had been beaten up at a meeting of the party in London's East End and he was banned from appearing on the BBC and ITV. After 1966, however, as time had passed and views had become more liberal, he began to appear on both channels, most notably on a *Panorama* programme in 1968 which attracted an audience of 8½ million. In the same year he published an autobiography, *My Life*, which sold well. Mosley by now was being regarded less as a national threat and more as an interesting historical figure. This view of him was emphasised even more when, in 1975, Robert Skidelsky brought out a biography of Mosley which was not only balanced but gave a fair appreciation of Mosley's thinking since the war.

Diana was not so lucky and her autobiographical book, *A Life of Contrasts*, was not well received since it included praise of Hitler and a failure to condemn some of the nastier elements of the Nazi regime, particularly anti-Semitism. This, coupled with her obviously comfortable life, did not make her an object of sympathy and influenced the reviewers' attitude to her book.

Away from the public eye, the Mosleys were now accepted by many people both in England and France; their family life was happy, they were on good terms with all their seven children and with Nancy, Pam and Debo, and the thaw in the relationship between Diana and Jessica must have been welcome, at least to Diana. Sydney's death, followed by Nancy's illness and death, brought the sisters closer than they had been since politics and war divided them. But this was not to last.

The publication of *Unity Mitford – A Quest*, the biography of Unity by David Pryce-Jones, once again led to division between the sisters. Jessica was largely in favour and Diana, Pam and Debo were very much against. This event and the connected one of the mislaid scrapbook is related in detail in Chapter 17, but it is particularly relevant to the activities of the Mitfords during the 1970s as it illustrates the grouping which the four remaining sisters tended to fall into after Nancy's death: Jessica would take one side of an argument; Debo, Diana and Pam would take another.

Debo, particularly, felt that it was too soon to tackle a book on someone so controversial and that any biographer would emphasise the aspects of Unity's life which had so mesmerised the press in the pre-war years and after her suicide attempt. She and the others wanted to remember Unity as Jessica had actually described her in *Hons and Rebels*: 'I loved Boud for her huge, glittering personality, for her rare breed of eccentricity, for a kind of loyalty to me which she preserved in spite of our now very real differences of outlook.'

The others also testify to these traits and to her originality and eccentricity – there really was no one like her; but Pryce-Jones focused on her relationship with Hitler and her life in Germany. He had done much research, including interviewing some of Unity's remaining German friends and some of the Mitford cousins, but after the book came out many claimed they had been misquoted. Jessica told the other sisters that she had agreed to speak to Pryce-Jones so that he would have her view of Unity, but even she was not entirely happy with what he had written. What would have made the picture of Unity more balanced was if Diana, Debo and Pam had agreed to speak to him, but they had refused. They were so angry when they saw the finished biography that they wrote a furious letter to *The Times*. Unfortunately, this and subsequent adverse publicity made people want to read the book and sales soared.

The incident almost caused a permanent rift between Jessica and her sisters, and it was only because of Debo's determination that this should not happen and Jessica's reluctance to sever the ties completely that the affair was patched up. Pam and Jessica were eventually 'on speakers' again, but Diana and Jessica did not build on the contact they had made during Nancy's illness and never saw one another again. It was left to Debo to keep the remaining family members up to date with the others' activities, as Sydney had once done. The fact that she took over this role irritated Jessica, since Debo was the youngest. The frustration of the others towards Jessica's attitude is not hard to understand and yet, rather like Unity, Jessica's personality when she was not involved in family disputes was warm and attractive, but she could be an implacable opponent on her many crusades, usually for good causes.

Debo herself had plenty of other things to occupy her time, most of them concerned with the survival of Chatsworth and to this end she created a quality gift shop, a farm shop, a butchery and a restaurant in the old stables. These enterprises, together with the charitable trust which Andrew had set up with the proceeds from the sale of some of the more valuable paintings in the Chatsworth collection, made the house a viable concern; it was to become, like its chatelaine, a national treasure. Debo also bred and successfully showed Shetland ponies, which she found to be a relaxation from the affairs of the house; like her father, shooting during the winter and fishing in summer were not only activities to look forward to, but emphasised the inevitable turning of the seasons which is precious to everyone who lives in and loves the country – and Debo is a true countrywoman.

Fourteen

Back on English Soil

Pam returned from Switzerland to live in England for good in 1972. She had enjoyed the years she spent in Switzerland but – true to form – had always said that she would return after the last of her dachshunds had died, as it wasn't kind to bring them back from 'the Continent' and introduce them to a new home in old age. In spite of Pam's love of 'the Gnomes', there was little to keep her in Switzerland any longer, though Giuditta chose to stay in Grüningen. There is no record of a rift between them; perhaps in the end each preferred to grow old in her own country.

Pam's house in Caudle Green, Woodfield, was currently let and while she waited for it to become available she stayed with Debo at Chatsworth in a flat with spectacular views across the park and christened 1A Chatsworth Buildings by Nancy. '[Pam] was the inspiration behind the making of the kitchen garden at Chatsworth. She had often talked of the possibilities of a neglected plot beyond the stables, known as the Paddocks, and a few years later it was transformed into the kitchen garden of my dreams,' writes Debo in her book *Wait for Me*.

Woodfield House, when Pam finally got there, was exactly right for her. It is set in 8 acres, with a garden at that time just waiting for her attention, outbuildings in which to keep the animals she acquired, and set on the edge of the village green where her neighbour Mr Mills looked after the cattle which she grazed upon it. The house itself is early eighteenth century with a much older barn, some of which is now part of the house, at the back. It was previously the home of the local GP, Dr Sanger, whose son Fred became the only man in the world to win the Nobel Prize twice, for chemistry, and who was voted Britain's most eminent living scientist. All the main rooms, including the attic (where Fred slept as a child and which Pam converted into a comfortable flat), have views over neighbouring Miserden Park, home of the Wills family, where Pam would walk for hours with Beetle, the black Labrador, who replaced the dachshunds. Beetle came from a litter of pups born at Chatsworth and was a dog of almost human mentality; his appearance was a great relief to Pam's family and friends who had found his small predecessors somewhat over the top. When he wanted Pam's attention he would tug the back of her skirt and lead her to whatever it was he needed at the time. Her good tweed skirts bore the marks of his attentions and when they became too ragged they were consigned to Beetle's bed because nothing Pam possessed was ever wasted.

Due to the weakness of her 'polio leg' Pam was uncertain that Woodfield would remain a suitable home for her old age and she resolved to convert a single-storey barn in her farmyard into a house. Unfortunately – as so often happens in the Cotswolds, an area of outstanding natural beauty – she fell foul of the planning authorities and also of two of her near neighbours; however everyone else in Caudle Green, where she was fast becoming a very popular member of the community, was quite happy for her to proceed.

One of the opposing neighbours, who lived in the only modern house in the village, which had a drive of red tarmac instead of the statutory Cotswold gravel, called to see her one day. 'Mrs Jackson,' he said, in his humourless Scottish voice, 'if you get planning permission for that barn I shall build a 20ft wall between you and me.'

'Oh, Mr Taylor, how wonderful!' replied Pam, fixing him with her blue-eyed smile. 'I shall grow a peach tree up my side. I've always wanted a peach tree.' She didn't get her permission – or her peach tree – but she certainly held the moral high ground.

The farmyard didn't remain empty: it became home to a rare breed of bantam, Appenzeller Spitzhaube, roughly translated as 'fluffy bonnets' because of the tasteful arrangement of feathers on their heads. They are white with black markings and were a familiar sight as they strutted about on the green. Books about the Mitfords say that Pam imported the breed into Britain from Switzerland. That is not strictly correct; 'smuggled' would be a more accurate word because in the early 1970s it was illegal to bring fertile eggs into Britain from Europe. This did not deter Pam in the slightest. She later told me that she simply put the eggs in an empty chocolate box (Swiss chocolates, of course), no doubt smiled sweetly at the customs officers and marched through customs with her precious parcel. The eggs were hatched out in an incubator at Chatsworth and another rare breed settled in the British Isles. Pam later contacted Joe Henson who had set up the Rare Breeds Survival Trust at his Cotswold Farm Park near Guiting Power, high on the Cotswolds. They became lifelong friends, no doubt enjoying each other's gentle sense of humour, as well as their passion for preserving rare breeds. How delighted she would be to see the high media profile that Joe's son Adam now has on the subjects of farming and rural affairs.

Still worried about impending lameness, Pam decided to make the house easier to manage, creating a large, comfortable living kitchen where she could cook, eat, sit, watch television and entertain her many friends. She also installed a pale-blue Rayburn cooker which, it was rumoured, she had specially painted to match the colour of her eyes. That simply wasn't her style. It certainly did match her eyes but this was merely coincidence – she liked pale blue. Any other explanation would suggest a vanity she did not possess.

When the builders had left, Pam needed someone to help her clear up after them and her great friend and neighbour, Dee Hancock, who lived on the other side of the green, suggested me. At the time I had a young family and had recently converted two formerly derelict cottages on the edge of the village. When Dee approached me I said

I would be delighted to help, especially as I had recently bought a donkey for my children and discovered that the price of hay had mysteriously leapt from 9p per bale to £1. I needed the money. What I didn't know at the time was that I was about to make a lifelong friend.

When I walked across Caudle Green to Woodfield House on a golden autumn morning, when the Cotswolds look their magnificent best, the name of my new employer, Pamela Jackson, meant nothing to me. Nor was I immediately alerted by the attractive, blue-eyed woman with the silver-grey hair and the distinctive up-market voice who came to the back door (nobody ever seemed to use the rather grand front door) and greeted me warmly. Nevertheless, I was an avid reader of both literature and history and as Pam showed me around the house, I couldn't help noticing that there were all the novels and biographies by Nancy Mitford on the bookshelves or on occasional tables, plus the satirical writings of Jessica Mitford. The penny began to drop. This was one of the Mitford sisters whose extraordinary activities and remarkable books had been familiar to me all my adult life. Why had I not heard of her before?

For the next ten years I worked for Pam and could never quite get used to the idea that the books which I dusted were mainly by Pam's family and friends, from her grandfather's *Tales of Old Japan*, to the latest offerings by Diana, Lady Mosley, and later by Deborah, Duchess of Devonshire and chatelaine of Chatsworth House. And there were books by Evelyn Waugh, a lifelong family friend, by poet laureate John Betjeman, Pam's loyal admirer of long ago, by Lytton Strachey, whom she had known when managing Diana and Bryan Guinness's farm at Biddesden, and many others, including a slim volume of poems by Bryan Guinness himself with whom Pam had always kept on friendly terms.

Photographs of family members by Cecil Beaton and a drawing of Derek Jackson by Sir William Rothenstein were a further fascination, not to mention the pictures by Renoir and Delacroix which Pam was left by her close German friend Rudi von St Paul, née Simolin. 'I'm going to hang them on the wall, Diana, no thief would think of looking for them there,' she said. And she was right. The thief who broke in when she was away and stole easily disposable electrical goods left Renoir's still life of a bowl of peaches and Delacroix's dingy battle scene still hanging in the drawing room. Rudi and Pam had managed to smuggle much of Rudi's art collection out of Germany while they were still able to do so. They simply took the paintings out of their frames, packed them in their luggage and took them to Ireland where they remained until Rudi's death. It could be claimed that gentle Pam, who looked so innocent, became quite a practised smuggler.

Pam's sense of humour, though not the razor-sharp wit of some of her sisters, appealed to me. Pam knew this and always had some funny story to relate; like the time when Diana, Lady Mosley's book entitled *Loved Ones* was published. 'She wanted to call it *Dead Ones*, you know, because they all are, but the publisher thought it wouldn't sell.' Many of the stories were against herself and she was never afraid to tell these, especially if she felt they would cause amusement. One of the funniest Pam stories, which caused hysteria among the sisters, is related in Debo's autobiography *Wait for Me*. It happened at the wedding dinner of Debo's son Peregrine, now the Duke of Devonshire, to Amanda Heywood-Lonsdale. Pam was seated next to Lord Mountbatten who had been briefed on who she was; but it had not been thought necessary to tell Pam the identity of her high-profile neighbour. 'I believe you are called Woman by your family,' he said. She turned to him, giving him the benefit of her bright blue eyes: 'Oh yes, I am, and may I ask who you are?' The great man had no answer to this and turned to his other dinner partner. Hearing of this afterwards, Debo was incredulous that Pam had not known who he was. 'Well, if he had got all his medals on I might have recognised him,' she replied, quite unabashed. 'One of the wonderful things about Pam was how unimpressed she remained by names, money, titles, reputations or any of the world's extras attached to some people,' said Debo, the sister who probably knew her best of all.

As well as Beetle and the Appenzellers, Pam also had a goat called Snowdrop who was completely white with amber eyes. Snowdrop went for walks with Pam and Beetle and she would skip on to the top of the Cotswold stone walls when a car came past, much to the amusement of the driver. Often they would be joined on their walks by me and my two girls, Kate and Emily, riding Dusty the donkey and Gwenny, the Welsh mountain pony which we had recently added to our own menagerie. The road out of Caudle Green is a narrow one and the combination of two adults, a donkey, a pony, a dog and a goat made passing by an oncoming vehicle almost impossible. When a vehicle did approach, everyone except Snowdrop (who made for the wall) crowded onto the verge. The most likely person to be passing was Mike Fitzpatrick, the farm foreman for Miserden Estate; the first time he spied this strange group he wound down his window and asked: 'What have you done with the Ark?' After that he just smiled. What else was there to say? Pam loved it.

Later, Pam took possession of Minor, a miniature Shetland pony from Chatsworth, where Debo, among all her other activities, bred Shetlands. Minor was incredibly naughty (perhaps that was why he was with Pam and no longer at Chatsworth) but Pam loved him dearly and he did have his uses. One of these was to pull fallen tree trunks out of the wood at the end of Pam's garden. My family would be asked to help and have a share of the wood. Pam would harness Minor, attach long chains to his harness and then to a piece of tree trunk which Brian, my husband, had sawn to a suitable length. Then, with much verbal encouragement from Pam and a smack on his amble rump, Minor would rear up, exerting his full strength, until finally the trunk began to move and he trotted triumphantly out of the wood pulling his prize behind him. It was an exhausting experience, not only for Minor, and it would probably have been much quicker just to carry the logs; but it was a lot of fun and Pam was in her element. These were exactly the sort of activities which she had enjoyed all her life and for which she never lost her infectious enthusiasm.

Once back at Woodfield House, Pam and Debo saw a lot of one another. They were the two sisters who most enjoyed country life and Debo loved her visits to Caudle Green. Her particular recollection is the delicious smell of herbs – which she always associated with Pam, wherever she lived – as one opened the back door and walked towards the kitchen, and the single bedroom where she usually slept and where

Lark Rise to Candleford was on the bedside table for at least twenty years. All her life Pam was a natural homemaker and a wonderful cook but it was at Woodfield that she really came into her own and her kitchen garden was a sight to behold; she would grow exotic vegetables like kohl rabi long before they were generally heard of in England.

In the garden, she was helped by her neighbour Gerald Stewart who, along with his wife Gladys, became her dear friend. Sadly she didn't live to read Gerald's evocative account of his life, *Pipe Lids and Hedgehogs*, in which he describes life in the Cotswolds seventy-five years ago, but she would have been delighted to know that he was supported in this venture by her niece, Lady Emma Tennant, to whom she left Woodfield House. Emma's tenants, Stephen and Freddie Freer, would be just the people Pam would have chosen had she been let-ting the house and it was Freddie who persuaded Gerald to write the book. Thanks to his efforts and their enthusiasm the garden is almost exactly as it was when Pam tended it – a fitting memorial to this most rural Mitford.

Though Pam lived alone at Woodfield she had many visitors. Debo came the most often but Diana, Lady Mosley, also visited, captivat-ing everyone she met with her incredible niceness and charm which was such a contrast to the political views which she never renounced. Others who came often were George Budd and his wife Margaret. They had been Pam's close friends ever since George and Derek were stationed in RAF 604 Squadron together during the war; and it was Margaret with whom Pam was staying in April 1994 when she had the fall which led to her death – she could have been with no better person. Another visitor was Christopher Hammersley, the son of Mrs Ham, one of the subjects of Diana Mosley's *Loved Ones*. She had played an important part in the childhood of the young Mitfords who teased her unmercifully (which she loved) but also used her as a treasured confidante.

The coming and going of guests meant that, as well as my clean-ing duties, I had plenty of beds to change. Pam was not prepared to spend a lot of money on laundry: she washed the single sheets her-self but those from the huge double bed in her large guest bedroom were taken to Mrs Bird in the next village, who passed them on to the Paramount Laundry. 'I always remind her that I am an Old Age Pensioner because I get one shilling off the price of each sheet,' she would tell me with pride.

The sheets were not always laundered after each guest, however. When I arrived to change the big bed – always hoping that I would not have to turn the enormous flocked mattress which had a life of its own and would spitefully try to smother anyone who tried to turn it unaided – Pam would announce, if her sisters' visits were in close proximity: 'Debo is coming to stay next week and Diana will be here in two weeks' time, so one of them can sleep on this side and the other on that.' When one sister had left, Pam would stand on one side of the bed and me on the other, and we would tug the creases out of the side which had been slept in. This was not an easy task since these sheets were Irish linen (what else?) and creased very easily. If the sisters knew about this it must have amused them greatly; it was just one more example of Woman's 'carefulness'.

Other family guests included Pam's nephew, Max Mosley, and his family. Despite her later confession to her sisters that she felt she had not always shown enough affection to Max and his brother Alexander when they were living with her at Rignell as babies, Max very obviously had a great affection for Aunt Pam. But Pam always felt that the family would be bored by her company and would march them up the village to my house where Max, who was at the time heavily involved in developing the March racing car, would get into deep conversation with my husband Brian who had pioneered the sports racing car, the TVR V8, while all the children raced around the large, untidy (compared to Pam's) garden.

Debo, who probably knew her better than anybody, says in *Wait for Me* that she thinks Woodfield was Pam's happiest home. 'It was the ideal house for anyone who loves the Cotswolds. Pam's presence there felt exactly right: the house, garden, paddocks and owner all suited each other.'

Fifteen

Living the Life She Loved

*P*am happily settled into the even tenor of life which Caudle Green offered and became one of the village's most popular residents – not because she had a title (very few people except the postmen, Maurice, Tony and Ron, realised that she was the Hon. Pamela Jackson) but because she was, simply, nice.

One of her closest friends was Dee Hancock who, with her husband Johnny, lived in the big, Georgian-fronted farmhouse across the green. Although they only got to know one another when Pam came to live in Caudle Green, Dee had long known of the family (who didn't?) because in her brother's diary, written while aboard his battleship during the war, she had found an entry which read, 'the Mitford girls came to tea'. Also, she remembered that her grandfather Sir Albert Muntz had known the then Duke of Devonshire and the Mitfords' grandfather, the first Lord Redesdale, because they were three of the most well-known Shire horse breeders of their day. When Dee, Debo and Pam all went to the Royal Show, where the grandfathers had exhibited their horses, they felt that they were reliving the past. Dee recalled:

Also, my brother was killed in the war and I didn't find it easy to talk about it, but when Pam described the terrible sense of loss that Derek felt at the death of his twin brother Vivian I found that I could tell her my feelings too.

Pam was a really good friend to me. She had been through a lot herself and was a very understanding listener but she was also very original and good fun. Although she suffered from what I used to call 'workhouseitis' and couldn't bear to waste anything – she ate rabbit bran for breakfast – she was also very generous, always sharing the exotic vegetables which she grew in the garden – and she even lent me a dress to wear to Buckingham Palace.

Our friendship could have been severely tested on the occasions when the cattle which she grazed on the green escaped onto the road and she would hail Johnny and me to come and help her – usually when we were in the middle of dinner. But we were such good friends that it never mattered.

Mary Sager was a Yorkshirewoman with a wry sense of humour and many was the evening when she and Pam had supper in her tiny cottage or when they walked together with Beetle in Miserden Park. Another Beetle-walker was Margery Clements who lived on the edge of the village in a cottage refurbished by Norman Jewson, a leading member of the Arts and Crafts movement, who was one of her friends. She led a very frugal life, existing mainly on bread and cheese, and was so thin that Pam used to refer to her as the Mythical Figure. When Mrs Clements left Caudle Green, aged 90, to live in the much more remote Cotswold village of Temple Guiting, she sold her cottage to Michael and Pat Moody, who also became good friends of Pam. Pat said:

I was born in the 1930s, and that was when Pam lost a baby and never had any more. I didn't get on with my own mother and I often used to wonder if I was meant to be Pam's daughter because I grew to love her so much. For ages after she died I would wake up in the night and cry because I remembered she wasn't there. I always felt a great sense of affinity with her.

One day I asked her if she was going on holiday and she told me she was off to Switzerland. She must have been about 84 at the time and she was driving there all on her own. When she got back I asked her if she had had a good time. 'It was lovely, but I was sad that I couldn't fit in any swimming,' she told me.

Pam confessed to Pat that she had a terrible fear of fire which stemmed from a time when she was out to dinner and the stables of the house caught fire. 'We formed a human chain in our evening gowns and poured water on the flames. Luckily we rescued all the horses.' Could some of this fear also date back to when, as a little girl, she had reported a smell of burning but had not been believed and as a result the house which the family was renting was destroyed?

Pam often spent Christmas at Chatsworth and on one occasion she told Pat and I, well in advance, that this was going to be a white Christmas. 'How do you know?' we asked incredulously, wondering if long-range weather forecasting was yet another of her undiscovered gifts. 'Well, it will just be Debo, Andrew and one or two other old people and we've all got white hair,' she replied.

Joan Sadler, former principal of Cheltenham Ladies' College, who came to live in the village not long before she retired, has an abiding memory of Pam: 'She ... once took me into her house and showed me a picture which had been painted by Hitler, hanging at the top of the stairs. Of course I knew he had been an artist, and it was a good painting, but I was absolutely flabbergasted.'

Julian Leeds, who had bought his house from Pam's old and treasured friend Mr Mills, remembers Pam and Beetle on the village green. He also recalls an incident which shows that she was nobody's fool. She had had the approach to her house resurfaced and the tarmac was still soft but somewhat rough. Margaret Budd and another friend were staying at the time and Pam persuaded them to spend most of the weekend tamping down the tarmac.

Despite the belief by her family that she 'wasn't good with staff', the three cleaning ladies whom Pam employed while she lived at Woodfield House were very fond of her and took it upon themselves to find another suitable person to clean for Pam when they left. During the time that I worked at Woodfield, I would sometimes recruit my friend Pat Saunders to help with big projects, like cleaning and polishing the huge tiled floor with Cardinal Red polish, which had to be used until there was not a single scrape left in the tin. When I left Caudle Green to live near Cirencester and to work on the local newspaper, Pat was my obvious successor.

Pat first found favour with Pam when she scrubbed the flagstones in the hall, a task which I had never thought to tackle. 'How wonderful!' exclaimed Pam, and Pat secured her place on the Woodfield team. Pat said afterwards:

> I absolutely loved working for her, we always had a joke and a laugh and I never went home without a smile on my face. I really enjoyed meeting her sisters – Lady Mosley and the Duchess were the ones who visited most. They were always very appreciative of the fact that I kept their rooms clean and tidy – I'm not sure if they knew that they were sharing the sheets, though.
>
> Pam was really upset when eventually I had to leave but then Di and I thought of Celia Fitzpatrick who had just given up her previous cleaning job and we persuaded her to take over.

Celia's husband Mike was the same farm foreman at the Miserden Estate who always found Pam's and my procession of animals walking up the lane so amusing. Since the couple lived in Caudle Green, Celia already knew Pam: 'I first met her when I went house-to-house collecting for the Arthritis Trust. I felt very shy and I didn't like doing it but Pam was very keen to give and also produced a cauliflower from her garden. I felt pretty good after that.'

Celia brought a new dimension to the job since she was very handy with her needle. She made loose covers for Pam's chairs and curtains for the comfortable flat which Pam created out of the attic rooms. 'I also took up one of Lady Mosley's skirts and later made a dress for her but I wasn't very comfortable with that because I wasn't really a dressmaker.'

Even in the 1980s, when most people had given up turning their sheets 'sides to middles', Pam's careful nature would not let her throw worn sheets away. Celia had the job of carefully renovating them, but even when they, too, had worn out they were still not completely discarded. Pam would make periodic visits to the hospital in nearby Cirencester where some unsuspecting receptionist was presented with a pile of ancient sheets for use among the patients. What became of them in an age of throwaway equipment is not known, but they were obviously graciously received because Pam always returned home with a smile on her face. 'They were *so* pleased to have them and said they would be very useful,' she would say.

'It was always "make do and mend" and I did a lot of the mending,' said Celia.

The one thing that none of the cleaning ladies was allowed to do was to dust the oak beams in Pam's bedroom because she didn't want the dust falling on the bed. Neither was she keen on them cleaning too often in her little writing room where she kept her family photographs because the carpet didn't fit properly and they ran the risk of making the situation worse by vacuuming too vigorously.

Celia enjoyed being among the many books and reading the ones which Pam lent her, particularly those about the adventures of her mother, Sydney, her aunts and uncles, and her grandfather Thomas Gibson Bowles during the time when they lived on their boat. She was also very keen on wildlife and loved to see the birds which visited Pam's bird table, including a pair of kingfishers. Pam would make cakes to give all her cleaning ladies and she was always keen to distribute recipes for cheap, nourishing meals like brisket and brawn. Celia remembered:

Once, when we couldn't leave the village by car after a heavy snowfall, Mike brought milk and bread back by tractor from Miserden but he also went to see if he could bring anything else home for anyone. He was somewhat nonplussed when Pam said she would like some sauerkraut but, determined not to be beaten, he managed to find some for her. She was always very kind to us and after Mike had had his stroke, I happened to mention that he needed something to put his feet up on. Next time I went she had found a footstool for him.

Pat, Celia and I are all agreed that working for Pam was a particularly happy time in our lives. 'She was a real one off. She told us all stories and jokes and loved to make us laugh. We loved her and we even loved the cleaning,' said Pat.

We also agree that the cleaning would have been much easier if Pam hadn't been so keen to preserve water, her attitude to which is best summed up in a conversation with her friend, the writer and aesthete James Lees-Milne:

> I never allow my daily to clean the bath because she wastes so much water. And another thing I strongly urge is, if you must run the hot water tap waiting for the water to get hot, always run it into a bucket or two, to be kept handy. Then you can take the buckets of tepid water downstairs and out into the vegetable garden where it will always be welcome.

This story was relayed by James Lees-Milne to Diana, who in turn put it in a letter to Debo. The sisters shrieked with laughter over it: 'Why water? It's as though she lived in Greece and dreaded the well giving out …' Yet the whole truth is even more astonishing. Pat and I both remember that Pam would have liked us to use cold water for the cleaning; it was us who persuaded her to let us run the lukewarm water into buckets and take it to the garden. In truth, water conservation was something Pam had learnt from her mother: Sydney had spent the greater part of her childhood sailing with her father, so she was always made aware that fresh water was a precious commodity and it is said that she would only pour herself half a glass at a time in order to ensure none was wasted.

Keen to do her bit for the village, which had received her with such open arms, Pam agreed to stand for the Brimpsfield Parish Council which included Caudle Green. Debo wrote to Diana from Lismore Castle:

I'd have given anything for you to have been here last night. Woman got out all her papers about standing for the Parish Council from her Unscratchable and Derek Parker Bowles teased her and made us die. She is truly wondair. She isn't going to be there for polling day neither has she canvassed a soul. Nevertheless she is referred to as Councillor Jackson and her advice is sought re everything from drains to foreign policy … She loves being teased by someone like that.

Since she didn't canvass, she didn't get in, which was probably just as well. Her humour and originality would probably have gone down like a lead balloon in the seriousness of local politics. (The Unscratchable in which she had carried her papers was an attaché case of fine leather which Pam would allow no one to touch in case it got scratched. It travelled in a cloth bag of its own so as not to be damaged.)

Much more successful was the Silver Jubilee party which she held in her cowshed and to which she invited the whole village. She wrote enthusiastically to Debo:

We are deep in our Jubilee Party arrangements. Just only the people of Caudle Green and it will be on the Monday because all the other parties are on the Tuesday. It will be a barbecue, Sausages from the Moncks [sic], rolls from the Nudist Colony!!! A real Cheddar Cheese in its own skin, a barrel of jolly beer, some of the Appenzeller eggs pickled in vinegar as one sees them in Pubs. There will be a bonfire and games, three-legged and sack races etc etc. And the room with the great west window (the cow shed) is to be tidied for the occasion – it's exactly what we need with light and water laid on!

Debo and Diana chuckled at the idea of holding a party in a farm building but it was exactly the right place; the party was a huge success, as Pam related to Diana, who in turn told Debo in a letter:

The farmer on the hill said no he wouldn't come and he was sure his sons had a party already, well one day before, he *caved* in and of course they all *loved* it. I knew they would. Most people said yes at once when they heard it was in my cow shed, but some said no, but in the end they all *caved* in. I just got hold of the monks and the nudists* for more sausages and rolls, we hung up tea towels everywhere and of course everyone *loved* it, and we lit our bonfire when the Queen lit hers. One man who had said no came in the end with two guests, he just *caved* in at the last moment. I knew he would, I said to Mr Mills, they are sure to want to come and of course they did. They just *caved* in.

Such enthusiasm was so infectious that Pam's Jubilee party was a talking point for weeks, and more than thirty years later my daughter Emily remembered her delight when she discovered that Pam had dyed some of the Appenzeller eggs red, white and blue for the occasion.

Another village gathering to which Pam went regularly was Tea Cups, started by her nearest neighbour Barbara Rowlands, who lived in what had once been the Woodfield House chauffeur's cottage. In fact, when Barbara decided to sell up and move into nearby Cheltenham, Pam bought the cottage which again became part of Woodfield and still belongs to Debo's daughter, Lady Emma Tennant, who inherited the estate. Tea Cups took place once a month during the winter in different houses in Caudle Green and everyone who lived there was invited. It was an excellent way of people keeping in touch during the bad weather when they were less likely to be walking on the green or in their gardens.

Pam took her turn in hosting Tea Cups at Woodfield and everyone enjoyed their visits to her large, cosy kitchen with its pale-blue Rayburn and highly polished tiled floor. She also enjoyed visiting the homes of her neighbours. 'I can still picture her sitting at the head of our table, drinking her cup of tea and I remember her telling us how when she and her sisters were out for a walk with Nanny in London,

---

* The monks came from Prinknash Abbey, near Painswick, and sold delicious home-made sausages; Pam didn't share Sydney's views on the consumption of pork products. The nudists were the inhabitants of the Whiteway colony, founded on Tolstoyan ideas of equality, on the far side of Miserden Park. If they ever bared their bodies, they no longer do so, but they are a somewhat eccentric community which at that time had its own bakery of which Sydney would certainly have approved.

they would ring the front door bells of the big houses and run away. They were obviously no different from village children,' said one of her neighbours, Christine Whitaker.

In 1977, the same year as the Silver Jubilee, Pam celebrated her 70th birthday. Diana and Debo hired a flat in Rutland Gate, close to where the family had spent time in London as children, and hosted a small party for her. In a letter to Jessica, describing the event, Debo wrote:

> It was like a Jubilee Street Party, squashed up like sardines. I think she rather loved it. Derek Jackson came all the way from Paris for the night, insisted on sitting next to her, huge bunch of red roses and VAST cheque as present, and he took her back to Claridges where they quaffed champagne till one in the morning. Do you think he'll marry her again?

Although she and Derek remained very good friends until the end of his life, Pam had now settled into a contented late middle age at Woodfield House, surrounded by her animals and her many friends. She would have been unwilling to change it even for the man who had been the love of her life.

She did, however, shortly before her 70th birthday, buy Riverside Cottage, opposite the Swan Inn at Swinbrook, as a precaution in case Woodfield became too much for her to manage. She rented it to various tenants and she and I would drive over (always with Pam at the wheel) to clean it every time a new tenant was due to arrive. She never lived there in the end; she was too content in Caudle Green. Instead, she created the flat in the attics at Woodfield and made sure every tenant was a strong young man who could chop logs, clear snow and generally help her to go on living there. Pam was nobody's fool and the arrangement suited everyone. She made many new young friends who insisted on inviting her to their dinner parties. 'Oh, Diana, you've no idea. They pour different wine into the same glass and sometimes even mix the wine if you haven't quite finished,' she once told me, raising her eyebrows in mock horror. But she would never refuse an invitation and she made a great impression on the young people she met, most of whom had never heard of the Mitford sisters.

Sixteen

Home Economics

O ne of Pam's characteristics which the other sisters joked about
was her homeliness, which manifested itself in her lifelong
love of cooking and eating good meals cooked either by herself or others. While the other sisters became prolific writers, Pam
never actually got round to putting pen to paper, though it had been
her intention to write a cookery book. Possibly because of her dys-
lexia, the thought of it became a burden to her. She had twice been
approached by publisher Jamie Hamilton to write the cookery book
and twice declined, after which, to her enormous relief, the editor at
Hamish Hamilton told her that there was probably no market for it.

She wrote to Diana in March 1982: 'For me one great worry has
been taken away – Mr Machell [the editor] says the cooking book
would be no good. I am deeply relieved and can now really relax, it
was such a hideous effort and I had to struggle to find time to do it.' It
was a burden which had been worrying her for some years. As early as
1966 Jessica is recorded as saying to Debo: 'We must get after Woman
about the cookery book.'

Some years earlier, when commenting to Debo on Diana's memoirs, she confessed: 'If I started my memoirs it would be nearly all

Food!' In the very same letter she talks about a lunch where she gave her guests *pot-au-feu*: 'I must admit it was delicious and *all* the guests had a second helping. I might give it to you and Andrew when you come.'

'She remembers meals 40, 50 years ago, even on the boat going to Canada,' said Debo to Diana; in this she was not entirely accurate for Pam even remembered meals from childhood and was ecstatic when the 'Super Cinema' came to Oxford – not because of the films she and her siblings might see, but because they could get supper there. When writing to Nancy for her birthday in October 1966, she says:

> Do you remember 42 years ago on my birthday at Asthall [she was 15] when there was such a heavy frost that the wire on the hen pens was quite closed with frost sparkles and the sun was shining brightly; Farve gave us all enough money to take the bus to Oxford and lunch and cinema. When we arrived we had ages to wait for lunch so as it was icy cold you insisted on going to the Ashmolean Museum, we were against it as it was costing sixpence each and we would not have so much lunch as we had hoped. However we agreed to go as it was the only place to keep warm till lunch time. Then, to our joy, we met Uncle George in the museum and he invited us all to a wonderful feast at Fullers!

This letter is well worth further examination, not only because it illustrates Pam's delight in food and her memory for long-ago meals (she could probably remember exactly what she and the others had eaten at Fullers), but because it shows that the sister who was thought not as bright as the others had a wonderful way with words. How easy it is to picture the bright, sharp coldness of the day, the teenage girls in a freezing Oxford street, arguing about what to do next; going into the Ashmolean, meeting Uncle George (their mother's eldest brother) and enjoying a wonderful warming lunch. Unlike Nancy and Jessica, Pam tells it exactly as it was, not trying to be funny or clever or endeavouring to appeal to a wider audience. What a pity she found writing such a burden because it would be fascinating to read her version of the Mitford childhood – as seen through her wide blue eyes.

Pam was never happier than when she went to Canada in 1929 with her parents on yet another of their unsuccessful gold prospecting expeditions. She and her mother kept house and cooked in the sturdy log cabin where there were few mod cons, no doubt making appetising dishes which would also be beneficial to the Good Body, including the wholemeal bread made to Lady Redesdale's own special recipe. She was the only one of the sisters to visit Swastika, since she was the one who most enjoyed both travelling and the simple life.

In the summer of 1939 Pam and Derek travelled to New York where he was on a high-level mission for the Air Ministry. While there they called in on Jessica and Esmond, who by this time were living in Greenwich; the sisters were delighted to see each other. Although Pam hadn't seen Jessica since she had run away to Spain almost three years earlier, as usual it was the food which she remembered most vividly. Writing to Jessica forty years later she reminded her that they had eaten roast chicken which Pam had carved and it was so hot that even the effort of carving it had brought her out in a 'muck sweat'. It was after this visit that Pam and Derek made their epic flight home in one of the first sea plane passenger flights.

Throughout her life, important events were best remembered by the food that had been made and consumed at the time. Rudi von St Paul, née Simolin, who had been the one to find Unity in a German hospital after her suicide attempt and who subsequently became one of Pam's closest friends, was equally keen on food and remembered meals which she had enjoyed. This was a trait which led Debo to refer to them as Professors of Past Menus, leading to screams of laughter from the other sisters. Unluckily for Rudi, nature was less kind to her than to Pam and she became very overweight in later life. 'Poor Rudi,' said Pam sadly, on hearing of her friend's death. 'How she abused her body.'

It was a pity that Rudi did not live to enjoy Pam's 80th birthday celebrations, arranged for her by Debo's husband Andrew at Brooks's club in London, where forty-three family and friends sat down to delicious food and wine in very congenial surroundings. Pam wrote to Jessica:

The dinner was Borsch soup, Saddle of Lamb, Profiteroles with hot chocolate sauce. Champagne before dinner, a lovely Meursault and then Leoville Barton and Champagne again with coffee. Everyone seemed to be enjoying themselves and were in top form. It was so good of Andrew to give such a party, I had expected to be here quietly.

Pam was more than capable of giving her own birthday party and cooking it all herself, as she had explained to Diana three years earlier. She had invited her cousins Rosemary Bailey and Madeau Stewart, plus her great-niece Catherine (Jonathan Guinness's daughter), Catherine's husband Jamie, Lord Neidpath, and their baby son Richard to lunch to celebrate her 77th birthday. 'The menu is to be Roast Leg of Lamb (from Chatsworth), chicory and red chicory salad and one other veg, Aura potatoes and then Apple Charlotte and various cheeses and I am already in a worry that it won't be ready in time! Catherine is such a good cook.' There is no record of how the party went but there can be no doubt that it was a great success. When Pam dined with the Neidpaths at Stanway House, near Chipping Campden, she always had to remember to wear extra underwear since the dining room was beautiful but very cold.

Having the butchery at Chatsworth which Debo had recently set up, selling meat from the estate, meant that Pam always had access to excellent fresh meat. The snag was that she had no room to freeze a whole lamb so she would buy one and sell half of it to me. On one memorable occasion we had my mother-in-law, a former lady of the Raj, staying at our house. She then lived in a safe and leafy London suburb where the doors were always kept locked and visitors discouraged. One wet and stormy night she was sipping her first whisky and soda in our kitchen, waiting for the rest of the family to get changed for a visit to the cinema, when through the door burst a soaking wet vision in black mackintosh, black sou'wester, and black wellington boots, leading a black Labrador with one hand and holding a bag of raw meat in the other. 'Is Diana there?' asked the vision. 'Could you tell her it's Mrs Jackson and I've brought her lamb?' The subsequent cinema visit to an Alistair MacLean wartime adventure story was almost an anticlimax.

Aura potatoes were often the subject of Pam's jokes. Always up to date with the introduction of new types of vegetable, when Aura was put on the market, she was delighted. 'Oh, Diana,' she said, when I arrived to clean, 'I've always enjoyed Desiree potatoes because they make me think of Dee [Dee Hancock's real name was Desiree] and Dee's sister is Aura. Desiree and Aura, *both* with potatoes named after them!' This was a very 'Pam' joke. It had none of the cleverness of the other sisters but Pam's delight in it made me laugh and I remembered it thirty years later. It is somewhat reminiscent of a joke Pam heard many years previously at an Eton vs Harrow cricket match, while her brother Tom was still at Eton. In the evening after the match there was a concert, where a comedian regaled his audience with jokes, some about the schools. 'I've Eton College pudding and it's given me Harrowing pains' made Pam laugh hilariously, but it would not have raised as much as a smile from the others.

Stories about Pam and food were wrought in Mitford family history from the time the girls were still living with their parents. On one occasion a friend of Lady Redesdale had turned up unexpectedly for lunch and distracted her from the planning of the day's meals. The result was that rice was served twice at the same meal, first as risotto and then as rice pudding. 'It was ghoul, *two* rices at *one* meal,' Pam told Debo in horror. The incident was never forgotten and any disaster was referred to as 'two rices' in Pam's voice. Her dismay was only matched when instructing her cook on how to make game soup. She related the dreadful event to Debo: 'You know, Stublow, isn't GS the loveliest and richest soup you ever *laid hands on*. Well, a *milky affair* came up.'

She must also have been unsettled by a letter she once received from Debo who had 'Uncle Harold' Macmillan, the former British prime minister, to stay when he was very old.

Uncle Harold is being very good, what Nanny would have called No Trouble. Sometimes he gets up, sometimes he doesn't. When he stays in his room he has bread and butter for breakfast, lunch, tea and dinner. Yesterday he got up and had 2 helpings of curry at lunch and

2 pancakes after lots of other stuff at dinner. I can't imagine what his stomach must make of such contrasts.

Pam must have been horrified even to think of such a diet.

When travelling in Austria she remembered the food as clearly as the magnificent scenery. 'We had a most wonderful first course. It wasn't a soufflé and it wasn't an omelette, in a dish about that high,' she said, measuring two or three inches with her fingers. 'It was *so* delicious.' While staying with Diana in Paris she gave her neighbouring dinner table guest the benefit of her cooking knowledge by telling him in detail, in her rather halting French, how to deal with a certain cut of pork. To prevent any misunderstanding as to which cut should be used, she stood up and pointing to her own body pronounced: 'Il fait le couper LA.' ('You must cut it HERE.') During the same stay, Diana heard her advising other guests on the treatment of potatoes – 'Then you smash the potatoes in some of the best olive oil.'

'Isn't she one in a million?' wrote Diana to Debo.

Food was so much her domain among her less domestic sisters that Pam could be quite bossy about it. Diana was somewhat daunted by the idea of spending time with Pam when cooking was involved. In a letter to Debo in 1982, she wrote:

> I'm longing for my visit to Woman, but also *terrified* because she suggests we each cook every other day. First of all I can't, and second, imagine how I'd do every single thing WRONG, wrong times, wrong ingredients, wrong casseroles (the latter bound to be ruined if I cook them). Oh Debo do you think she would take me to Marks and Sparks and I could secretly buy all? … Can't you picture Woman and Beetle back from a walk and Woman saying 'I smell burning' or 'Nard, you should have put the potatoes on *long* ago.' It really will be the agony and the ecstasy because I love Woodfield and Woman and all but am not house trained.

However much they might laugh among themselves about Pam and her domesticity, they all enjoyed her cooking. Nancy, for instance, told Debo that Pam had cooked trout, chicken and sugared ham for various meals during a visit to Woodfield, and Debo later enthused to Nancy about a meal she and Diana had had with Pam as 'SUPREMO. Head Soup (out of) and Scotch Collops [were they scallops or a rare cut of meat?], no pouding [pudding]. Huge coal fire. Bottle of wine she had smuggled from France [more smuggling] ...' Nancy, however, was lucky to get any wine with the trout during her gastronomic visit. When Pam collected her from the station, she asked Nancy, 'Naunceling, air u toird?' (Nancy, are you tired?)

Nancy said, 'Oh, well, only rather.'

'Because if you're very tired I shan't give you some really lovely wine, it wouldn't be worth it.'

Nancy let out such a bellow of rage that Pam nearly ran into the ditch. But all was well. They drank the lovely wine and the dinner was *wondair*.

Head Soup which Debo had so enjoyed before the Scotch Collops was not made of a 'ghoul' (Pam's own word) collection of animals' brains as its name suggests. It was simply 'soup out of my head', as Pam would tell those who wanted the recipe; she could not give it to them because it was never quite the same – it depended what she decided to put in it or what she had in her larder and kitchen garden, but it was always delicious. She usually made the stock from a chicken carcase or a ham or lamb bone, but if she had none of those things to hand she would add water to what she called a 'K-norr stock cube'. To this would be added all manner of seasonal vegetables and herbs from her garden and the seasoning would often include Lea & Perrins Worcestershire sauce, nutmeg, lemon juice and a variety of other spices depending on the ingredients. When she was making it a most enticing smell pervaded her kitchen and it was always eaten with Lady Redesdale's wholemeal bread.

Her nephew, Max Mosley, has vivid childhood memories of her excellent cooking and also of her 'out of my head' recipes:

If one asked her where she got the recipe, she would usually answer 'I made it out of my head' which used to mean that as children, none of us dared catch the other's eye for fear of starting to laugh. And of course, we always asked for the recipe just to get her to say that, even in later life.

My principal memory of her is that she was a full-on food enthusiast. She would come back from a trip abroad and regale everyone, particularly my mother, with what she had eaten. 'The menu, Nard, was the following ...' was heard so often that it became a sort of catchphrase.

He also recalls that while living in Ireland, Pam would drive for miles to get the right pig's head with which to make brawn, one of her specialities.

Pam was never one to resist a challenge where cooking was concerned. While still living in Ireland she turned down an invitation from Debo to visit her at Lismore Castle because she was making egg mousse for sixty people, who were invited to the Tullamaine point-to-point. This could easily have been on the menu at the Royal Show in 1969 when Debo hired a stand and introduced her Haflinger horses, newly imported from Austria, to an admiring public. 'My sister Pam and I hired a caravan, parked it behind the horses' stalls and spent a week there. Pam made lunch for crowds of friends; we sat on straw bales and were entirely happy.' This would not have been regarded as fun by any of the other sisters, but for Pam and Debo it was exactly what they most enjoyed.

Both Debo and Pam were equally thrilled when Debo introduced the Duchess of Devonshire line of groceries to the Chatsworth shop and various other outlets early in 1987. Debo wrote to Pam:

I'm longing for you to see and taste the FOOD. We had 38 distributors (commercial travellers really) here on Wed, lunch for all, a tour in the freezing cold of the State Rooms etc, to try and show the fellows what we have to look after here ... Then we went to the Stag Parlour set up with chairs like a school room & THE PRODUCT was unveiled, along with various pots and tins from rival firms to show how much better ours are! I long to know what *you,* specially, will think of them.

Pam's main experience of brand products had been in 1976 when the village shop in neighbouring Brimpsfield had closed for good and she had bought all the remaining contents at a knockdown price – which must have pleased her greatly. But even she didn't get round to using everything up, because when Debo and one of her staff from Chatsworth went to clear her house after she died in 1994, they found and threw away many items from the larder, the oldest of which had a sell-by date of 1977. Of that time, Debo told Diana:

> Arriving here was awful ... It's odd beyond anything not to find her here. I've been faithfully round the garden plant by plant and am glad she can't see the precious new tree peony (expensive) which has been struck by a frost and the new growth hangs in that horrid way. I'm also glad she can't see the way we treat the water and the electric light, wickedly extravagant.

All through her life Pam just couldn't resist a bargain. In 1968 she announced to Nancy that she would be arriving for Christmas laden with household goods for her store cupboard. These included two 5kg drums of soap powder for the laundry machine, and she could, if necessary, get hold of first-class soap powder for the dishwasher, bird seed and maize, envelopes, floor cloths and loo paper (very soft) from Switzerland at much cheaper prices than in France. Nancy, who found simple domestic tasks like boiling eggs and washing saucepans quite beyond her capabilities, must have shuddered at the thought of all these bargains arriving at her elegant Paris flat, but it is most unlikely that she managed to deter Pam from her mission.

Pam's careful nature was at its peak many years earlier when Debo needed a cot and blankets for her youngest daughter Sophy when she went to stay at Lismore Castle for the first time. She felt sure that Pam would have not have thrown away the baby items she had acquired when she had had the Mosley boys to stay during the war, and she was right! Pam wrote from Tullamaine:

> Of course I will get you a cot, blankets, sheets & all. I have a *perfectly good cot* that Al and Max used at Rignell. If painted would it not save a

lot for you to borrow it while here? I think it may need a new mattress also a pillow. I have some *perfectly good blankets* which have a few moth holes; if Frau Feens [the seamstress at Lismore] cut them into the right size leaving out the *eaten parts* she could put some pretty ribbon to bind them and this would again save a lot. Then what kind of sheets, linen or cotton? If linen, I have some large double bed ones which are *rather worn* but here again Frau Feens could find plenty left to make cot sheets.

Debo forwarded the letter to Diana underlining the words now in italics. This was their sister at her 'make do and mend' best, the true heir to their mother Lady Redesdale.

Just occasionally, however, Pam was persuaded to part with some of her most elderly belongings: in the spring of 1989 she told Diana about a list of items she was having specially collected by the district council since they were too heavy for the usual dustbin round. It was a very long list ending with 'old metal feeding troughs, rusted and holy'.

Seventeen

Sisters, Sisters

*E*very large family has its changing relationships and with a family with such diverse views as the Mitfords, there was plenty of chopping and changing. Although sometimes infuriated with what one or another thought or felt, there is no doubt that they loved each other dearly. It was just sometimes hard to sympathise with someone whose views were so diametrically opposite to one's own.

As teenagers Unity and Jessica shared a bedroom and as their political views widened they drew a line down the middle, Jessica draping her half with the hammer and sickle and other left-wing propaganda, and Unity displaying the swastika and a selection of Nazi treasures on her side. They would shout slogans across the divide but they were firm friends and no one mourned Unity's death more than Jessica.

Nancy saw fit to shop Diana to the government when war broke out and was instrumental in her and Sir Oswald Mosley going to prison. She also suggested that Pam and Derek were fascist sympathisers, which was far from the mark. Yet when she was dying of cancer it was Pam and Diana who looked after her.

For much of their adult lives Diana and Jessica were on 'non-speakers', though Diana had been Jessica's favourite sister as a child.

They did not meet or communicate after Jessica's disappearance to Spain and Diana's marriage to Mosley until Nancy was dying, and even then there was much discussion as to how the meeting should be arranged. Debo, being the youngest (there were sixteen years between her and Nancy), was not so much involved with the early squabbles and in later life became the family peacemaker. Tom, during his short life, was wise enough not to take up the cudgels with any of his sisters; nor was it in his nature to do so.

An incident in 1962 illustrates how, in spite of all that had happened to them during their colourful lives, they still held firm to the differing views of their childhood. One day in August Pam and Giuditta arrived to stay with Diana in Paris, giving her only three hours' notice of their arrival. Diana and Sir O, as the sisters often called him, were going out and so Pam and Giuditta went to see Nancy with whom Jessica was staying – at this time Jessica never saw Diana when in Paris, but she did keep up her relationship with Nancy. When Diana, Mosley, Pam and Giuditta all met again at the end of the evening, Diana was aware that the visit had been a disaster and that Pam and Giuditta were very upset. 'What can have gone wrong?' wrote Diana to Debo.

She soon discovered. Before she and Giuditta went home to Switzerland, Pam described how the conversation at Nancy's had turned to their old family friend Violet Hammersley. It was a well-known fact that Mrs Ham's two sons, Christopher and David, were her favourites and that her daughter Monica had had a miserable childhood, being mainly ignored by her mother. 'Well, that's just like our miserable childhoods,' chorused Nancy and Jessica, much to Pam's dismay. 'It's not TRUE,' she said to Diana, her blue eyes filling with tears, and Diana agreed. Even in their fifties, the sisters still looked back to their childhood in entirely different ways, with Diana, Pam and Debo always seeing the good side of their parents and remembering all the happy times, and Nancy and Jessica (who would probably have been joined by Unity) convinced that they had been deprived and ignored. This is perhaps further illustrated by the fact that the three malcontents' great ambition was to go to boarding school while the home lovers, especially Diana, confessed to feeling physically sick at the thought of it. To add insult to injury, neither Nancy nor Jessica had spoken a word to Giuditta during the whole of the evening, which had further upset Pam. 'We smoothed them down and they went off fairly happy I think,' Diana told Debo, but one cannot imagine Pam, Diana or Debo behaving so rudely.

Since Pam was uninterested in politics and never espoused causes as her sisters did, she was usually on good terms with all the others, who tended to regard this completely different sibling with mild amusement. Having been at the sharp end of Nancy's cruel teasing for most of her childhood, she had learned to keep her head down and in later life, when she had forged her own kindly if eccentric character, she never tried to compete with any of her sisters.

In their letters to one another, the others often have some joke about Pam and her domestic interests and careful nature, both inherited from their mother. Nancy wrote to one of the others saying that Pam had been to London for the white sales: 'How can she be my sister? I've never been to a white sale in my life and I hope I never have to go to one.' During a visit to Italy, Jessica wrote to Nancy:

Woman arrived here yesterday! She is thinking of writing a book because 1) you and I got so reech [rich] from same, and 2) she has masses of boxes of writing paper left over from when she was married to Derek and it seems a shame to let it go to waste. She seems in v. good fettle. I *am* glad she could come as I haven't seen her for years.

It was Jessica, however, with whom Pam had a 'non-speakers' period which started in September 1976 and went on for several months. Of all the sisters, Jessica was the most likely to take offence and spent much of her life in conflict with her family. This was partly because she was the one who lived a completely different life with her husband and children in California and partly because she had always been a rebel.

In 1976 journalist, novelist and biographer David Pryce-Jones was writing a biography of Unity to which Pam, Diana and Debo were opposed. Jessica, however, who had exchanged houses with Pryce-Jones in the summer of 1970, had given him help with the book, telling him about the sister to whom she was closest and never stopped loving despite their extraordinary differences. The other sisters hated the book, which Pam described as 'pornographic', and were angry with Jessica for her co-operation. When a large family scrapbook which had been at Chatsworth mysteriously disappeared, Pam wrote to Jessica suggesting that she had taken it and used it to help Pryce-Jones with his research, also letting him use some photos from their mother's album.

Knowing Pam's generally mild nature and reading the letter more than thirty years later, it seems surprising that it caused such a furore. But Jessica was as incandescent as only she could be:

Woman, [not dear or darling Woman] I was absolutely enraged by your *foul* letter implying that I've stolen Debo's scrapbook and given P-J photos from one of Muv's scrapbooks. As you well know, Muv left all hers to Jonathan Guinness so why don't you get after him. I have practically no photos of Bobo [Unity], and have given none to P-J. There are, obviously, huge amounts to be had in newspaper offices & I suppose that is how he got them.

And on and on justifying herself; she even sent a copy of the letter to Debo.

The row went on, with Jessica repeating her present grievances and bringing up more from the past, Debo trying to keep the peace and Diana feeling powerless to help because of her long estrangement from Jessica, but basically taking Pam's side. Through all this Pam seems to have kept calm but, as we have seen already, she felt things very deeply yet had learned through years of Nancy's teasing not to show her true feelings. Neither does it seem at all likely that she intended to cause such conflict within the family. It simply was not her style. The truth was probably that, as she was not herself quick to take offence, she had not – possibly naively – expected Jessica to react in the way that she did.

Jessica was further incensed when Pam later wrote to her but didn't mention her previous letter and that, when the book miraculously turned up at Chatsworth, where presumably it had been all the time, Pam didn't apologise for accusing her of taking it. Without wishing to make excuses for Pam, Jessica was not one to apologise for any of her behaviour towards the family, particularly the unsympathetic way in which she portrayed their parents in *Hons and Rebels*. Once the scrapbook was found Jessica wrote to Pam saying that she would like to see her again but could never forget her original accusation. It's impossible to see Pam taking the same stance if the situations had been reversed.

They met for dinner in Burford, near their family home, in December 1976, and appear to have made some sort of peace. Certainly, a year later Pam wrote to Jessica saying how much she had enjoyed her latest book, *A Fine Old Conflict*, and obviously felt on good enough terms to pick her up on several points. She reminded Jessica that she (Pam) had not broken her leg when accosted by Nancy, disguised as a tramp, while the two were running a cafe for strike-breakers on the Oxford road in 1926; she had only sprained her ankle. She also took Jessica to task for saying that she couldn't return to England after her husband Esmond had been killed because all the family had been pro-Nazi.

> This was a sad figment of your imagination, what about Nancy, rabid anti-Nazi and always announced she was a socialist, Debo, Andrew, Tom, Derek and myself? We had all very much hoped you would return and I thought it was probably because of the very hazardous journey that you decided not to do so.

On this subject, it has to be said that although not pro-Nazi as such, Debo, Andrew, Tom, Pam and Derek were all right wing by the standards of the day and would certainly have seemed so to left-wing Jessica, who perhaps, on this occasion, had a point.

In their defence, although it at first seems a little unfair that the three sisters thought Jessica had taken the scrapbook, it was an incident in the past which encouraged them to doubt her. When Sir Oswald Mosley stood for Parliament in 1959, Jessica wrote a letter to a friend saying how sorry she was that she could find no photo of Mosley with Hitler or Mussolini just to remind people what he was like. She added – and it was not entirely a joke – 'I guess that leaves it up to us to steam some out of Muv's scrapbooks at the Island. I do hope she won't mind.'

Pam and Diana remained close all their lives. Pam's polio and different temperament meant that she could never keep up with Nancy, and although Diana was three years younger, the two girls were educated together and played together – when Pam was not inventing solitary games of her own. When Diana married Bryan Guinness Pam ran their farm at Biddesden and remained friendly with Bryan all his life. She also got on well with Mosley and kept in close touch with Diana so that when the Mosleys were imprisoned at the beginning of the war for their pro-Nazi sympathies, it was Pam who took in their two baby sons, together with Nanny Higgs. Pam's nephews stayed with her and Derek for eighteen months at Rignell Hall, along with their two half-brothers, Jonathan and Desmond Guinness, when they were not at school or with their father.

Many years later, after Pam confessed that she could have been more affectionate towards the two boys, Diana and Debo bewailed the fact that the children could not have gone to another member of the family. But who? Their mother was Unity's full-time carer, Debo at the time did not have a permanent home of her own, Nancy simply would not have coped and Jessica, even if she had lived in England, was not an option.

Pam was the obvious choice and it says a great deal for her strength of character that she was able to admit to her feelings so many years later. It also seems a little churlish of the other sisters to keep on about something she couldn't help and which had happened so long ago, even if it was true. Apart from running the risk of being labelled a fascist herself, which probably bothered her not a jot, she must have performed miracles to keep her ever-increasing household fed and clothed after the introduction of rationing. She also had her mother and Unity to stay, which Unity always loved, and at Christmas 1941 she had eight to Christmas lunch and was worried that they wouldn't have enough to eat. Of course, she managed as she always did.

Diana felt that Pam had been insensitive when she had had her dog, Grousy, and mare, Edna May, put down while she was in Holloway. She thought Pam had had no idea of how upset she would be. But Pam had had to sacrifice the herd of cattle that she had bred, including the bull, Black Hussar, because she could no longer get food for them. She knew exactly how painful such decisions were, but it was wartime, the Mosleys were in prison, and Pam had their children and their animals at a very difficult time.

In any case, although Pam may not have been at her best with babies and toddlers, she was a tremendous success with older children whom she never patronised but treated as adults with ideas of their own. Lady Emma Tennant, her eldest niece, is adamant about her rapport with older children and teenagers; as am I – my children absolutely loved her.

It was Pam's relationship with Nancy which was the most complex and which really moulded the character she became. Nancy's admission that Pam's birth was one of the worst moments of her life was not a frivolous one. She made Pam's life miserable for most of their childhood, not only teasing her cruelly but picking on her, rather than the others, because she was the least able to defend herself. Looking back over both their lives, it could be said that Nancy had done Pam a favour because, through Nancy's treatment, Pam developed a character which was at least as strong if not stronger than her sisters', yet she still retained her kindly, sensible nature.

This character meant that she led a much happier life than Nancy, for whom, aside from her brilliant writing, things never quite worked out. Her relationship with Hamish Erskine was a disaster, her marriage to Peter Rodd was a mistake from the beginning and her love affair with her French colonel, Gaston Palewski, never resulted in marriage – instead he married someone else while still seeing Nancy. Her books brought her success and fame but somehow she never seemed to be really happy and she never wanted to return to live in England.

Pam, however, never lost her joy and enthusiasm for life. It comes through in her letters and in the memories of all who knew her. In the latter part of her life Nancy enjoyed fame and fortune, she lived in Versailles, which she loved, she wore beautiful designer clothes and enjoyed the company of many witty friends; but contentment was not really in her nature. Pam, on the other hand, was still the 'unknown Mitford sister' who returned to the Cotswold countryside she loved so much and enjoyed old age clad in 'good tweed skirts' with her dog at her side and her friends and family around her.

It was fortunate that when Nancy was diagnosed with cancer in 1969 Pam was able to help look after her. Diana, living in Paris, was able to visit Nancy most often but she was also looking after the ageing Mosley, and while Debo was very keen to help she had many commitments at Chatsworth and with her family. Although Pam at the time was living in Switzerland, she had no family ties there – except her dogs – and it was her visits which Nancy looked forward to most and Pam whom she most needed when she felt really ill. The others could make her laugh and have fun with her but when she wanted to cry, 'Woman is so perfect … she puts things right in a second.' Pam took her to the hairdresser to boost her morale, cooked delicious meals when she felt she could eat them and latterly dealt with the more humiliating parts of serious illness, like bedpans.

In her gentle way she made Nancy laugh with memories of their childhood. 'Wooms is being so truly wondair,' wrote Diana to Debo after the hairdresser visit. And when Nancy had a new cook who didn't come up to the mark, Diana wrote again: 'The only real answer is Woman,' adding, 'Naunce says you and I are for fair weather only, and I said no, for foul too, and she says no, only Woo for foul.'

It was Pam who accompanied Nancy to Germany to research her book on Frederick the Great. 'Woman was the heroine. I shall never go away without her again,' wrote Nancy to Debo on her return in October 1969. In the following March she wrote to Jessica: 'Woman is still here – she has been awfully ill but has come to now. I wish to goodness she would settle in for our old ages but don't like to suggest it. Her company suits me exactly – but people must have their own lives I know, furniture, pictures and so on (worst of all, dogs).' It was all a very far cry from their childhood days when Pam was constantly at the receiving end of Nancy's bullying.

It is tempting to think that Pam, with her womanly qualities and her natural nursing skills, felt very much in her element during Nancy's illness. But although Pam was happy to do all she could for her sister and enjoyed her company, she did not enjoy staying in Nancy's smart but uncomfortable and draughty flat in Versailles and longed first for her cosy little house in Switzerland and later for Woodfield, where she returned during Nancy's illness. Nancy, though she was much less sharp when she had Pam to look after her, was often in pain and must have been difficult to live with. Also, by this time Pam was over 60 and was making frequent journeys from either Switzerland or England. She never seemed to age or tire, but the constant driving, much as she enjoyed it, must have taken its toll. In a letter to Debo dated shortly after Pam's death, Diana writes:

> When Naunce died she [Pam] said, 'Nard, let's face it, she's ruined four years of our lives.' Poor Woo, how she *hated* Versailles and I expect Naunce blew hot and cold, in fact I know she did. Oh Debo! Her best and happiest years were Biddesden, Rignell and above all Chatsworth, Woodfield and YOU.

Diana, of course, was right. The sister to whom Pam was the closest was Debo, in spite of the age gap of thirteen years, which meant that they did not really share a childhood. Unlike the others they were true countrywomen, rejoicing in their love of the land and of animals, especially horses which they both knew a great deal about. Unlike the others they enjoyed living in the various country houses which, due to their father's fluctuating fortunes, became their homes. Neither craved the bright lights of town life and simply enjoyed being at home. 'We would have died if we had had to go to boarding school,' said Debo, still remembering the horror of that idea at the age of 90.

Pam spent a lot of time at Chatsworth, to which her great contribution was the making of the kitchen garden; Debo was delighted with it and wrote to tell her so. Debo also stayed often at Woodfield and the two could be seen walking with Beetle along the Cotswold lanes. When Debo was modernising the Devonshire Arms, a hotel belonging to her husband's family in the heart of the Yorkshire moors, Pam was at her side to help and would return home to give her friends enthusiastic blow-by-blow accounts of the alterations. I remember these in detail and I can't help feeling that Debo must have missed Pam's company, though not necessarily her ideas on interior design, when she later gave the Swan Inn at Swinbrook similar treatment. The pub had been left to the sisters by an elderly lady in the village and Debo has filled it with fascinating Mitford memorabilia which Pam would so have loved.

In 1984 Pam took Debo and her younger daughter Sophy on a trip to Swinbrook, Asthall and Batsford to show Sophy where her mother and aunts had spent their childhood. They were warmly received and one can imagine Pam's pleasure at showing her niece her childhood haunts. They would also have seen the family gravestones in Swinbrook churchyard, including the one which Pam organised for Nancy. Carved at the top of the slab of Cotswold stone is a mole, reminiscent of the moles which appear on the Redesdale coat of arms. One of the sisters happened to remark that it looked more like a baby elephant galloping across the gravestone, which caused shrieks of laughter among the others.

Pam enormously enjoyed the annual game fair at Chatsworth and took great interest in all the innovations which Debo introduced to the house and estate, especially the restaurant and the food shop. The sisters visited the Royal Show regularly and also went to Smithfield, where Debo served her turn as president.

'[Pam] was the complete countrywoman. Her life revolved round the kitchen garden, kitchen, her dogs and also her car. She had enormous courage which she inherited from our mother,' said Debo, who confessed that Pam was the only one who still told her what to do, even in their old age.

Eighteen

Almost the Final Chapter

While Pam was enjoying rural life in Gloucestershire, her sisters' lives also continued along the lines of the last two decades but with some marked changes, due to the fact that the Mitford Girls, once an icon for extravagantly behaved youth, were getting older.

The first casualty in the family was Sir Oswald Mosley who, until his late seventies, had remained active and energetic. After his 80th birthday in 1976 he aged quickly. He had Parkinson's disease and the pills he took for it often caused him to fall over. For the first time in his life he began to look his age, although he still made occasional television appearances; he was due to fly to London to take part in a television programme when he died peacefully in his bed in November 1980.

For Diana it was as if part of her had died too. He had been her whole life for almost half a century. She had given up nearly everything for him and, although she had managed to pursue a literary career – she had just completed a biography of the Duchess of Windsor before Mosley died – her main aims were to convince him that he still had something important to contribute to the world, to defend his ideals and to look after his physical needs. The fact he had little influence on political thinking after the war did not matter; she would back him to the hilt and this included her unrepentant attitude towards Nazi Germany. She supported him willingly because she never stopped loving him, and for him, in spite of his early philandering, she was the love of his life.

Her sisters were not entirely surprised when, the following year, Diana had what at first appeared to be a stroke but was, in fact, a brain tumour. She was flown to a London hospital where the tumour, which turned out to be benign, was removed and she made a complete recovery, greatly helped by a period of convalescence with Debo at Chatsworth and a later holiday with Pam in the peace of Caudle Green. In hospital she had many visitors of which one of the most regular was Lord Longford. 'Frank's so faithful. Of course he thinks I'm Myra Hindley,' she joked with her family.

The sisters' lives were now calm in comparison to what they had once been but public interest in them did not diminish. In the early 1980s television presenter Julian Jebb made a documentary entitled *Nancy Mitford – A Portrait by her Sisters* to coincide with a dramatisation of *Love in a Cold Climate* and *The Pursuit of Love*. Pam was the star of the programme, with Diana and Debo appearing somewhat stiff and awkward in comparison, but old family differences had also come to the fore once again; Jessica insisted she would only appear on the programme if Jebb included a letter from Nancy which claimed that Tom had only pretended to be a fascist. Once again Diana, Debo and Pam protested, but the item about Tom had little impact on the viewing public and the programme was a success. Jessica just could not resist these political pinpricks although she must have known that they would once again cause family ructions. Nevertheless, when Mosley died, although she could not bring herself to write to Diana directly, she asked Debo to give Diana her sympathy. Of all the sisters, she had, perhaps, the most mixed up loyalties.

Another family row, this time among the Mosleys, blew up in 1983 when Mosley's son Nicholas produced *Rules of the Game* which highlighted his father's infidelity to his mother Cimmie, and the distress this caused her. The rest of the family was up in arms but the book was published just the same. The following year, Jonathan Guinness and his daughter Catherine produced *The House of Mitford*, the definitive history of the family, but Jessica refused to co-operate partly because she did not get on with Jonathan and could not understand how Catherine could deeply love her grandmother Diana when she knew what she believed in.

In 1984 Jessica had a minor stroke while on a lecture tour to South America. She recovered well and tried to give up the heavy smoking and drinking which she felt must have contributed to it. However, it was not until she fell and badly broke her ankle in 1994 that she gave up alcohol altogether, realising that the fall was the result of having too much to drink. She did it by sheer willpower, confounding her family and friends. Possibly the sudden and unexpected death of Pam as the result of a fall (though it was not alcohol related) in the April of that year brought her face to face with her own mortality.

Jessica's broken ankle was giving her trouble so she went to the doctor, where she also mentioned the fact that she was coughing up blood. Lung cancer was diagnosed and this quickly spread to her liver, kidneys and brain. An operation was out of the question and she was given three months to live. In fact, she lived for less than six weeks. She spent her last few days at home looked after by Dinky, now a qualified nurse, who had fully lived up to her mother's early description of her as being just like Pam. The funeral was minimal, as befitted the author of *The American Way of Death*, but there were two enormous memorial services: one in San Francisco and the other in a London theatre, led by Jon Snow who had become a friend. Debo was asked to speak but in the end could not face the razzmatazz 'so stayed at home with my own thoughts about my remarkable dear old Hen'.

In only two years the four remaining sisters had been reduced to two, and Diana and Debo grew even closer, keeping up a constant correspondence until Diana's death in 2003. Diana had brought out her last book, *Loved Ones*, in 1985 which contained pen portraits of family and friends, including Mosley, Mrs Ham and Derek Jackson, and she continued to write book reviews, notably for the *Evening Standard*. As she grew increasingly deaf, the letters and faxes between the two sisters increased since they could no longer chat on the telephone, a source of sorrow to both of these lifelong natterers.

Diana was never in the shadows for long. Her life with Mosley and the beliefs she still held made sure of that. In November 1989 she appeared on *Desert Island Discs* on which she refused to condemn Hitler or admit that Mosley was anti-Semitic. This caused a national outcry from both the general public and the Jewish community, but Diana remained unrepentant. Jessica, of course, was filled with righteous indignation that Diana should be allowed by the BBC to air her views at all.

Diana never got used to life without Mosley and some of her letters to Debo reveal her great sadness and loneliness in spite of the attention of her loving children and grandchildren. She finally moved from the Temple de la Gloire to a flat in the heart of Paris and it was there that she died of a stroke in the heatwave of 2003. She was 93 and completely confounded the prediction of the nanny all those years ago that she was too beautiful to live long.

Debo, the much-teased youngest sister whose birth went so unregarded and who Nancy said could only read nine words, really came into her own in the dying decades of the twentieth century. Apart from being 'one of those Mitford sisters', she had already made a name for herself as the mistress and saviour of Chatsworth. In 1982 she, too, burst into print: 'I began writing at Uncle Harold's [the former Tory prime minister] bidding. He was looking for the Handbook of Chatsworth and Hardwick, written in 1844 by the Bachelor Duke. He said, "You ought to write what has happened to the house and garden since." So I did.'

That is the story of Debo's whole life; ideas and opportunities have presented themselves and she has risen to the challenge.

The result of Uncle Harold's suggestion was *The House: A Portrait of Chatsworth*, published in 1982, which was an instant success and sold many copies. Always the businesswoman and realising she had found a winning formula, she followed this with *The Estate: a View from Chatsworth* and *Chatsworth: The House*, a sequel to her first book. With these books she demonstrates that she has the same flair for writing as her sisters – would that Nancy had lived to see the day when Nine would also become a respected writer. Her other books include *Counting My Chickens and Other Home Thoughts*, *The Duchess of Devonshire's Chatsworth Cookery Book*, no doubt partly inspired by Pam, *Memories of Andrew Devonshire* and *Home to Roost and Other Peckings*. Her autobiography, *Wait for Me*, published in 2010 when she was 90, received enormous publicity and spent several weeks in the bestseller lists. Unlike Nancy's novels and Jessica's 'biographical' books, Debo, true to form, tells the story of her family exactly as it was.

As well as running Chatsworth and taking up her pen, Debo has undertaken many other projects. These include hosting the Chatsworth Game Fair, the Chatsworth Horse Trials and the International Sheepdog Trials, becoming a non-executive director of Tarmac, and president of the Royal Agricultural Society of England. In 1997, aged 77, she went on the Countryside Alliance march in London accompanied by her younger daughter, Sophy. Having completely renovated the Devonshire Arms at Bolton Abbey in Yorkshire in the 1980s, she set about doing the same to the Swan Inn at Swinbrook when she was in her late eighties. Her talent for organisation is undoubtedly inherited from the Bowles rather than the Redesdale side of the family and her determination to keep her often-at-odds sisters together is Sydney all over again.

Her passion for Elvis Presley seems an odd one for an elderly duchess but it is very real. She has visited Graceland – and loved it, including the bizarre decor – and in her present home, the Old Vicarage at Edensor, she has an Elvis room and an Elvis telephone.

However, life has not always been plain sailing for this most energetic of the Mitford sisters. Alcoholism ran in the Cavendish family – Andrew's father's early death is thought to have been hastened by the habit – and Andrew also became an alcoholic, his mood changes making life very difficult for Debo and their family. After several fruitless attempts to give up, he finally succeeded with the help of Debo and his children, and until his death twenty years later, he never touched alcohol again.

Andrew died in 2004 and Debo later moved into the Old Vicarage, leaving her son, Peregrine, always known as Stoker, and his wife Amanda to run the Chatsworth estate.

Five of the Mitford sisters lived extraordinary lives by anyone's standards: Nancy, the French Lady Writer whose lover was de Gaulle's right-hand man; Diana, who married British fascist Sir Oswald Mosley at a ceremony in Goebbels' dining room and in the presence of Hitler; Unity, the friend of Hitler who shot herself rather than see England and Germany in conflict; Jessica, who ran away with Churchill's cousin to join the communists in the Spanish Civil War and became a respected left-wing journalist in America; and Deborah, friend of the Kennedy family, who became the Duchess of Devonshire and saved her family's stately home against all the odds. You simply couldn't make it up.

But at the centre of this story is Pam. Pam, who was never responsible for a headline beginning 'Peer's daughter …'; kind, ordinary Pam who put up with terrible teasing from the others but looked after them when they were sick or sad; Woman, who was teased for her carefulness but envied for her culinary skills; and Tante Femme, so called by Debo's children, who was loved by her nephews and nieces because she never patronised them. She had no wish to emulate her colourful siblings, never sought the limelight and was perhaps the only one who was entirely comfortable being herself. She is mentioned in the numerous books about the sisters which constitute part of the Mitford Industry, but no one before has cast her in the starring role. She would be amazed to find herself centre stage. 'How extrorder,' she would giggle, her forget-me-not blue eyes wide with surprise.

I have called this 'Almost the Final Chapter' for three reasons. Firstly, due to its chronological position; secondly, because the end of the Mitford family story will, of course, come with Debo's death. But thirdly, and to judge from past history, it is a story which will never actually end because fascination with this family, whose exploits even the most imaginative writer of fiction would find it difficult to invent, just goes on and on.

Nineteen

Contented Old Age

The last years of Pam's life were contented and happy. She loved living at Woodfield House and had plenty of help in the house and garden. She saw a lot of her family and her friends, many of whom came to stay. She particularly enjoyed the visits of her nieces and nephews and she found older children were drawn to her. Diana's son Max always kept in touch with her and remembers what fun it was to stay with her both as a child and an adult. 'She was very kind to us and is greatly missed,' he said.

Debo's elder daughter, Lady Emma Tennant, who loved her aunt dearly, is clear that when it came to dealing with children, Pam was always kind and natural, never patronising them and always treating them as adults. After Pam died, Emma's daughter Stella said that Pam was always a good person to ask for advice because she was so strong and sensible. The last family member to see Pam before her sudden death was Emma's elder daughter Isabel, who took her baby to visit Pam in the London hospital where she had had an operation on a broken leg.

Pam took an interest in the names which the younger members of the family passed on to the next generation. In 1993 she wrote to

Debo: 'I wish Sophy [Debo's youngest daughter had called her son Declan] had a nicer name for the baby, it sounds like something out of arithmetic or out of Latin. Isn't there a lesson on Latin – declining?' And her easy way with children was not confined to her own family. I well remember outings with my own children, organised by Pam. Especially memorable was a trip to Chatsworth to collect Beetle the Labrador, who always went to Debo (who had bred him) when Pam was away. Despite my offers to share the driving, Pam insisted on driving both ways on the same day – a trip of well over 200 miles. This included several delays because Emily kept feeling sick and Pam insisted on stopping each time and talking her for a walk to get some fresh air. She gave us a splendid day at Chatsworth, taking us into the family's part of the house as well as showing us the magnificent rooms which are open to the public.

The latter years of Pam's life had an extra tranquillity, because since Nancy's long illness when Pam had been the sister who could give her the most comfort, both in practical ways and because of her innately sympathetic nature, there had been no more teasing. Finally, the other sisters realised her true worth and her stature in the family was never questioned again.

Jessica, in a letter to Debo a few days after Pam's unexpected death, mentioned the teasing. 'Actually, I think she rather thrived on it,' she wrote. Whose conscience was she trying to salve? In Jessica's defence, she does go on to say what an utter trooper Pam had been when caring for Nancy and how it changed the way in which the rest of the family regarded her.

She also states that in spite of their quarrel over the lost scrapbook, after which they were on 'non-speakers' for several months: 'In recent years we became great friends, Bob and I adored going there, she used to come to parties in London … All my friends loved meeting her and vice-versa, I think.' And that was the joy of Pam – she was so particularly loveable. Her wide blue eyes were often invisible when she laughed hilariously at some joke, possibly even her own. And her calm, natural manner and practical nature endeared her to all those whom she met. She also developed a very strong personality (which may well have been a result of all the teasing) which made her most resemble the Mitford Girls' mother, Lady Redesdale. She never tried to compete with the others, was never glib or brittle as Nancy or Jessica could be; she was always herself. Her nephew Max says of her: 'She used to sort of slightly send herself up. She was fully aware of what amused the others about her and played up to it.' Her sense of humour was never far below the surface.

Life had not always been kind to Pam but she bore the bad times with the fortitude that was so much part of her nature. In spite of all the teasing, she was a happy child, finding pleasure in the country life that most of the others couldn't wait to get away from. She made light of it when her engagement to Togo Watney was broken off, but according to Debo it made her miserable. When her marriage to Derek Jackson came to an end after fourteen years she seemed to accept the fact with her customary calm, while underneath she was deeply unhappy. When Margaret Budd stayed with Pam at Tullamaine shortly after Derek had left, Margaret told Pam that she admired her enormously for staying so cool in the circumstances. 'If only you knew,' Pam replied, 'I may seem calm but everything is churning underneath.' At this time Derek was very cruel to her but he couldn't resist her kind nature for very long and they were soon friends again, remaining so until the end of his life. When he died in 1982 he left her a large enough sum of money in American dollars for her to write in a letter to Diana: 'I shall be so well off and won't know myself.' She added, typically: 'What is so terribly sad is the fact that I shall never be able to thank him. It quite haunts me.'

When Derek abandoned her, initially she had to live a much more modest life; she had no children but was never bitter or sorry for herself. Her naturally happy nature got her through the tragedies of her life. 'She was a saintly person and she radiated goodness,' said her niece Emma, remembering also her loyalty, courage and common sense. These qualities were particularly demonstrated when Emma held an exhibition in a London art gallery; the private view took place on a night of dreadful weather and many of her friends who lived in and around London didn't turn up. She was beginning to feel a bit let down by this when through the door marched Pam. She had driven from Gloucestershire just to be there.

Pam's personality and special qualities came to public notice during the late 1970s and early 1980s when the Mitford Industry was at its peak. In 1980, when director Julian Jebb made the television programme *Nancy Mitford – a Portrait by her Sisters*, Pam completely stole the show. She is shown at home at Woodfield in front of her pale-blue Rayburn and also at Swinbrook, where she stands by the Windrush river reading Nancy's description of Uncle Matthew and the chubb-fuddler from *The Pursuit of Love*. Aged 73 she became a star performer, simply by being herself. After seeing the finished film Debo wrote to Jessica: 'You will SCREAM – Woman's the star, absolutely at ease … Diana and I are v. boringly discreet, I look like a headmistress about to retire and sit absolutely still … Honks looks 1,000 which she doesn't in real life.'

At a similar time a television serial of *The Pursuit of Love* and *Love in a Cold Climate* was made and much of it was, appropriately, shot in the Cotswolds; some at Rendcomb College, a public school near Cirencester. Pam, accompanied by Beetle, was a frequent visitor on the set and was welcomed as a valued member of the team. Certainly no one regarded her as an interfering old lady and she gave authentic advice in her authentic Mitford voice. When the series appeared on television she invited Kate, Emily and me, since we did not possess a television, to watch the programme with her. All three of us were aware of the extraordinary situation in which we found ourselves – watching a television serial based on a famous family in the home of a member of that family.

I had also spent the evening of the 1979 general election watching the television with Pam. Margaret Thatcher had achieved a landslide victory and Pam, a lifelong Conservative, was ecstatic – as were many people following the Winter of Discontent. I was far more entertained by the descriptions by Pam of former Labour MPs who were losing their seats. 'Oh, look, Diana, Mr —— looks just like a white rat that we used to have as children', and, 'Oh, Diana, there's the white rat again!'

Another example of the Mitford Industry at this time was a musical entitled *The Mitford Girls*, a frothy and light-hearted look at the lives of this remarkable family, directed by Ned Sherrin. It took place at the Chichester Theatre, and Pam, Diana and Debo were invited to the opening night. When Pam returned I was keen to hear about the evening. 'Did the rest of the audience know you were there?' I asked. 'Well,' replied Pam, 'they couldn't really help it because all the gels in the chorus had badges which said "I am a Mitford Gel" but Ned had had special badges made for us. They were huge and they read, "I really AM a Mitford Gel."' She loved it.

A decade later, in 1993, the Mitford bandwagon was still rolling and a selection of Nancy's letters was published under the title of *Love from Nancy*. In a letter to Pam at the time of publication, Diana wrote: 'Don't we all sound horrible in the book. Except you.' Even though Nancy had spent a lifetime teasing Pam, she recognised what a particularly special person she was and always had been.

During the 1980s Pam and Diana became very close and spent holidays together, in Switzerland and Italy in the summer and South Africa in the winter. Pam drove them both on the European journeys, negotiating the terrifying Paris Périphérique without a map. But as she had feared would happen she became increasingly lame in the right leg which had been affected by polio when she was a child.

As early as 1978 she had written to Jessica, taking her to task for saying in her latest book, *A Fine Old Conflict*, that she had broken a leg while escaping from Nancy at the roadside canteen in 1926. 'So far, luckily, I have not broken a leg although I may well do so one day as I fall about like a ninepin.' These turned out to be prophetic words.

Although Pam had never allowed the weakness in her right leg to affect her life, as she grew older it began to take its toll, putting a strain on both her spine and on the left leg. During the 1980s she made several visits to Cheltenham-based orthopaedic surgeon Guy Rooker. As something of a Mitford sister watcher, he was very interested to meet her and he was not disappointed, finding her as delightful as everyone else did. He prescribed physiotherapy and anti-inflammatory medication and she also went for treatment to Cirencester physiotherapist

Deirdre Waddell. Typically, although she was keen to continue the treatment, Pam could not do so at the time since she was busy helping to look after Diana, who was recovering from an operation for what turned out to be a benign brain tumour. She later continued with the physiotherapy, finding that it did ease the pain.

The year 1987 was one that was both sad and happy. Beetle, who had become increasingly doddery, was put down in June, after much soul-searching. It was the end of an era for Pam who had never been without a dog and Beetle was much missed by Pam's neighbours since he had become so much a part of the village scene. 'I can so imagine how you miss sweet Beetle,' wrote Diana, 'but I'm sure his life had become a burden to him as well as to you. I only wish that when that happens to one, one could "send for the vet." So wonderfully easy.'

In November of that year Pam celebrated her 80th birthday, for which Debo's husband Andrew organised a party at Brooks's club in London. Many of her old friends, such as James Lees-Milne, were invited and lots of cousins, including musician Madeau Stewart to whom Pam had become particularly close. Pam described the event in a letter to Jessica:

> We were 43 altogether I think. It was all a great success. Lovely company, delicious food and marvellous wine and in a most beautiful room. Everyone seemed to be enjoying themselves and were in top form. It was so good of Andrew to give such a party. I expected to be here, [at Woodfield] quietly. Oddly enough I feel just as I did before I was 80 – somehow I had expected some magical change to take place but all is as usual!

According to guests at the party, Pam, in a gold lame jacket, her eyes as blue as ever, looked far younger than her 80 years.

Her neighbours would not let her birthday pass without their own celebration and organised a splendid tea party at Woodfield House. Very few were able to sit down with their tea and every room on the ground floor was full of people trying to balance tea cups and cake plates. Dee Hancock and I, meeting in the sitting room (the one with the ill-fitting carpet, not usually open to visitors), agreed that it was an enormous tribute to Pam that so many people had turned up.

In the late 1980s Pam's knees began to give her a lot of pain, in spite of spending winters with Diana in the warmth of South Africa which helped to ease her aching joints. By the spring of 1990 her right knee had become much worse and the following year, on 8 June 1991, Mr Rooker replaced the knee joint. The operation was a success and she went to Chatsworth to convalesce for three weeks and then to France to visit Diana at Orsay. From here she sent Mr Rooker a postcard of Diana's magically beautiful home, Le Temple de la Gloire:

> This is my sister's house where I am staying for a week, luckily glorious weather and we have seen many friends who are absolutely amazed at how well I can walk again, quite different from last year. And I have had no difficulties in the journeys, air and train. I had to tell you. With grateful thanks. Yours sincerely, Pamela Jackson.

Guy Rooker never forgot her and described her to me many years later as 'a nice, gentle, aristocratic lady who seemed to be perfectly content with being the least high profile of the Mitford sisters'.

Deirdre Waddell, the physiotherapist who treated her throughout this period, remembers her vividly:

> She was a charming lady, thoughtful and kind. She never came for treatment empty-handed – she would bring mint jelly from Chatsworth which she knew my husband loved, or soft fruit from her garden.
>
> She was always so grateful to the people who treated her and she regaled us with stories of her extraordinary family. She made an enormous impression on me.

In fact, after the operation's initial success she must have regressed somewhat, for in 1993 she wrote to Debo mocking her lack of mobility, demonstrating her usual ability to see the funny side of life, even in the face of adversity:

> I wish you could have seen us two travelling and in Zurich. As Nard [Diana] says we make one person: she can't hear but can walk, I can hear but can't walk. The result is that she rushes ahead and I can't call to her if anything important happens. Our compartment on the train was a quarter of a mile up the platform – she was there before I was half way! She carried the bags as I can't carry a thing with two sticks, only my bag slung round my Kneck.

In Mitford-speak, 'please picture'. By this time she was 86; it was eighty-three years since she had had polio and she was on her way to Switzerland. By anyone's standards, she was doing pretty well.

The following year, on 7 March 1994, Pam wrote to Jessica to say she didn't think she would manage a trip to California to see her and her family because 'I am getting very wobbly, not as agile as when you were here in the autumn and I fall very easily. It would be awful if I broke something when in America … I would love to see America again but honestly the old legs are beyond it now alas.' It was one of the last letters she wrote.

A month later she drove to London to stay with her old friend Margaret Budd. On 8 April they had been shopping, had dinner with their friend Elizabeth Winn, and afterwards gone for a drink with Margaret's next-door neighbour. Pam then did what she had always dreaded: fell down some steep steps and broke her right leg, the weak one, in two places below the knee. The ambulance men came quickly and she was given drugs for the pain and taken to hospital; the following morning she had an operation to put a metal plate in the leg. She woke from the anaesthetic asking, 'Who won the Grand National?' and appeared to be making good progress. She had a lot of visitors and was reported by Elizabeth Winn to be 'in fine form and very funny'; but the following Tuesday, just before Debo, who had returned from Ireland, could visit her, she died of an embolism to the heart.

The sisters were devastated. Suddenly Pam, who had been the constant rock in all their lives, who had been the butt of their teasing but who had always been there to comfort them when life was hard, had gone. She was 86, but her sisters had never considered life without her. Lady Emma Tennant, in her excellent obituary in *The Independent*, wrote:

> She never wrote a book, took up a cause or made headlines. Instead she lived quietly in the country, surrounded by the friends and animals she loved so much. They loved her in turn, and many people of all ages will find her calm, wise and deeply humorous presence irreplaceable in their lives.

She concluded:

> In old age, Tante Femme radiated serenity and goodness. Her huge blue eyes were as innocent as a child's. Indeed, innocence along with courage, honesty and cheerfulness was one of her remarkable qualities. But it was the innocence of a woman who had lived and suffered, loved and lost, and overcome adversity to enjoy an unusually contented old age.

The funeral was held at Swinbrook on a sunny April day, when the daffodils were blooming and the trees were just coming into leaf. The church was packed with mourners from every walk of life, whose lives in some way Pam had touched. They sang 'Eternal Father Strong to Save' which was one of her favourites. It had been sung every Sunday at Batsford, where the sisters had lived as young children, ever since their Uncle Tommy had come home on leave during the Great War, shortly after the Battle of Jutland; he had been enraged to find that there was no mention of sailors in the church service. Toby Tennant, Emma's husband, read from Ecclesiastes, Chapter III, and the sisters thought the verse 'Every man should eat and drink, and enjoy the good of all his labour, it is the gift of God' was particularly appropriate. Debo, like her father, deplored long sermons, so there was no sermon at all. There was no need for one; everyone there knew Pam's very special qualities.

Spilling out into the graveyard, I did a quick headcount of Pam's neighbours and hoped no burglar was abroad in Caudle Green that day as nearly every house would be empty. Even former neighbours, now living miles away, had come to say their goodbyes.

Pam was buried near the graves of Nancy, Unity and now Diana. Madeau Stewart planted lavender bushes on the grave and now lies beside her cousin and friend. The inscription on the simple Cotswold stone headstone reads, 'Pamela Jackson, née Mitford, 1907–1994, "a valiant heart"'. Those three simple words sum her up exactly.

But perhaps Debo, the sister to whom Pam was closest, should have the final word: 'There'll never be anyone remotely like her, will there?'

The Story of the Brooch

Towards the end of his stint as a navigator with Bomber Command, Derek Jackson commissioned Bond Street jeweller Cartier to make a brooch for Pam of the regimental insignia of 604 Squadron. It was a fabulous piece of jewellery made of diamonds, sapphires and rubies, and Pam kept it all her life and wore it often.

After she died, Debo, who took charge of her jewellery, at first considered donating it to a museum; she approached the RAF Museum and also St Clement Dane's church, which has an exhibition of RAF memorabilia. Both declined the offer, feeling that it was of too great a value to be on public display; so Debo lent it to Pam's very close friend Margaret Budd, whose husband George had been in the RAF with Derek.

Margaret kept the brooch for over a decade but when she reached the age of 90 she felt that she should pass it on to someone younger who would also treasure it. Debo suggested that it should go to Rose Jackson, Derek's only child and the daughter of Janetta Kee, his third wife. Although Rose had been estranged from Derek for most of his life, when he was old and in poor health they were reconciled and he became devoted both to her and to her little boy, Rollo.

Rose was thrilled with this precious gift and wrote to Margaret Budd on 5 October 2009:

Dear Margaret Budd,

I can't thank you enough for giving me Derek's squadron's – I mean Pamela's – brooch. It's a magnificent thing and above all it really reminds me of Derek. I can imagine him commissioning the piece and insisting on a very precise 'interpretation' of the Squadron's regimental badge.

It must have meant a lot to you. I expect it brought back memories of that time of your life and you would have known Derek and Pamela well then. Of course you lived through those many terrifying months when your husband and Derek flew.

I have none of those memories, but Derek did talk to me about his life during the war so it's wonderful to have an object to connect me to all of that.

I have 3 sons and it is a fascinating object to them as well. I shall take great pleasure in wearing it. Thank you so much.

With kind regards and best wishes

Rose, née Jackson, now Campbell

It was a stroke of genius from Debo. It may seem strange to some that such a special and sentimental object was given to the child of the woman for whom Pam's husband had left her, but that sort of jealousy was not in Pam's nature; she would have been delighted.

Pam's Recipes

LADY REDESDALE'S BREAD

4.5 cups wholewheat flour
1.5 cups bread flour
20fl. oz water
2 tbsp sugar
2 packets dried yeast (14g)
1 tbsp salt

Method:
Grease two baking tins. Place the water in a large bowl and add the other ingredients. Mix and knead the dough until it is thoroughly amalgamated. Leave in bowl to ferment for one hour. Remove dough from bowl, place on baking board and divide into two pieces. Shape the dough into rectangles the size of the tins and put into the tins. Heat the oven to 400°F/205°C. Cover the tins and let the dough rise for 30 minutes. Bake in the oven for 35 minutes. Remove loaves from oven and from tins and allow to cool on racks.

Pam made this bread all her adult life. It is delicious with butter, with jam, in sandwiches or just on its own with home-made soup. Although Pam seldom used an electric mixer, one can be used to mix and knead the dough for about 6 minutes at maximum speed.

SORREL & LETTUCE SOUP

2 handfuls sorrel
2 handfuls lettuce
Good bunch of parsley
2oz butter
4oz potato, peeled and diced
1pt chicken stock
Salt and black pepper
4 tbsp single cream

Wash sorrel, lettuce and parsley, then shake out and dry in a towel. Chop up roughly. Heat butter in a heavy saucepan, then add the three green vegetables. Stew gently for 5 or 6 minutes, then add diced potato. Stir well, then add hot stock. Cover and simmer gently for 25–30 minutes. Push through a food mill and re-heat in a clean saucepan. Season with salt and pepper, stir in cream and serve. (Serves 4)
Tip: Eat with Lady Redesdale's Bread

EGG MOUSSE

8 hard–boiled eggs
¼pt water
1 tbsp tomato ketchup
1 tbsp Worcester sauce
3 tbsp double cream
Salt and pepper
1 tbsp aspic powder melted in the ¼pt of water

Method:

Pass yolks of eggs through sieve; add ketchup and Worcester sauce, salt, pepper and half the aspic. Chop whites and add to the mixture. Finally, add cream. Mix well. Turn into soufflé dish and put in fridge. When set pour over the remainder of aspic. Decorate and leave to set.

This recipe was found in the cookery book of Pam's great friend Margaret Budd, but it bears all the hallmarks of Pam's imaginative cooking, like the addition of tomato ketchup and Worcester sauce for extra flavour. It is probably the recipe she used – much expanded – soon after she and Derek moved to Ireland and she told Debo that she couldn't come to see her at Lismore Castle that day because she was making egg mousse for sixty people at the Tullamaine point-to-point. And there is no doubt that the eggs would have come from her own hens.

POT-AU-FEU

4lb forequarter flank of beef or silverside, or 2lb of each
A piece of knuckle of veal weighing about 2lb including bone, if available
A beef marrow bone sawn into short lengths
Chicken giblets or 6oz of ox liver in one piece
4 large leeks
4 large carrots
2 large onions
1 very small turnip
Small piece of parsnip
1 stalk of celery with its leaves
Bouquet garni (2 bay leaves, 2–3 sprigs parsley and thyme)
1 tbsp coarse salt
8pt water

Method:
Put the beef, veal and giblets into a large cooking pot and pour over

the water. Bring to a simmer extremely slowly and keep skimming off the scum until it turns to a thin white foam which will disperse of its own accord. Add the vegetables, the bouquet and the salt. Put the lid on the pot, but tilt it gently so that steam can escape, and simmer very, very gently for 3½ hours. Add the marrow bone, tied up in grease-proof paper, and the liver and cook for another hour. Serve the beef with potatoes, freshly prepared vegetables and gravy made from the stock and keep the rest of the stock and the vegetables cooked in it for soup (perhaps Head Soup, see Chapter 16: Home Economics). Alternatively, the beef is delicious served cold with salad and baked potatoes or some of Lady Redesdale's bread.

This recipe owes a lot to one of Elizabeth David's in her book French Provincial Cooking, but Pam adapted it for her own use and would sometimes use brisket instead of flank for the main meat. She would also use the simmering oven of her Rayburn cooker instead of simmering the meat on the hotplate which gives an even better flavour. When making the soup Elizabeth David suggests that the marrow bone be extracted and spread on French bread baked golden in the oven. I think Lady Redesdale's bread, toasted, would be even nicer.

Acknowledgements

I should like to thank: Jonathan Guinness, Lord Moyne, for his help and encouragement and for writing the foreword to this book; Deborah, Duchess of Devonshire, for allowing me to use the Mitford Archive photographs and Helen Marchant for arranging this; Max Mosley and Lady Emma Tennant for talking to me about their much-loved aunt; and Dee Hancock for her unstinting interest and valuable information. Also the many other people who have so willingly contributed to this book. These include: William Cooper, Christopher Fear, Celia Fitzpatrick, Stephen and Freddie Freer, Lorna Gray, Julian Leeds, Pat Moodie, George and Margrit Powell, Guy Rooker, Michael Russell, Joan Sadler, Pat Saunders, Deirdre Waddell and Christine Whitaker.

I could not have written *The Other Mitford* without reference to the following books about the Mitford family:

The House of Mitford by Jonathan Guinness, *Letters Between Six Sisters* edited by Charlotte Mosley, *The Mitford Sisters* by Mary Lovell, *Wait for Me* by Deborah, Duchess of Devonshire and *As I was going to St Ives: A Life of Derek Jackson* by Simon Courtauld

Index